CORSI

TRAVEL GUIDE 2023-2024

YOUR SUSTAINABLE TRAVEL GUIDE TO CORSICA: AN ISLAND OF BEAUTY, ADVENTURE, AND CULTURE AND HISTORY

KIRAN MCDONALD

Corsica travel guide 2023-2024

Your sustainable travel guide to Corsica: An Island of Beauty, Adventure, and Culture and history

CORSICA

travel guide 2023 - 2024

Your sustainable travel guide to Corsica.
An island of Beauty, Adventure, and
history

INTRODUCTION..5

1. GEOGRAPHICAL OVERVIEW..............................7
    HISTORICAL SIGNIFICANCE............................. 11
    WHY TRAVEL TO CORSICA?............................. 14

2. PLANNING YOUR TRIP.................................. 17
    BEST TIME TO VISIT....................................17
    ENTRY AND VISA REQUIREMENTS...................23
    BUDGETING AND CURRENCY.......................... 25
    SPEAKING AND INTERACTION......................... 31

3. GETTING TO CORSICA................................. 34
    BY AIR (Flying to Corsica)...............................34
    GETTING TO CORSICA BY SEA 37
    TRANSPORTATION WITHIN CORSICA............... 40

4. CORSICAN REGIONS AND CITIES........................43
    AJACCIO: The Corsican Capital and Napoleon's
    Birthplace...43
    BASTIA...48
    CALVI...54
    BONIFACIO 59
    CORTE.. 63
    PORTO-VECCHIO...68

5. CORSICA'S ACCOMMODATION OPTIONS...........74

6. CUISINE AND DINING...................................79
    TRADITIONAL CORSICAN DISHES.....................82
    LOCAL FOOD MARKETS................................. 86
    DINING ETIQUETTES.....................................88

7. ACTIVITIES AND ATTRACTIONS........................92
    BEACHES AND WATERSPORT.......................... 92
    HIKING AND OUTDOOR ADVENTURES..............95

HISTORICAL SITES AND MUSEUMS................98

8. NATURE AND WILDLIFE....................... 102
CORSICAN NATIONAL PARKS.......................... 102
BIRDWATCHING AND NATURE RESERVES..... 105
MARINE LIFE AND SCUBA DIVING...................107

9. CORSICAN CULTURE AND TRADITIONS........... 111
LANGUAGE AND MUSIC...................................... 111
LOCAL ARTISANS AND CRAFTS....................... 113
CORSICAN FESTIVALS AND EVENTS.............. 116

10. PRACTICAL TIPS FOR TRAVELERS................ 119
SAFETY AND HEALTH.. 122
MONEY MATTERS...125
COMMUNICATION AND THE INTERNET........... 128

11. RECOMMENDED ITINERARIES......................... 131
ONE-WEEK CORSICAN ADVENTURE............... 135
FAMILY-FRIENDLY VACATIONS...........................137
ROMANTIC GETAWAY.. 139

12. USEFUL PHRASES AND VOCABULARY.......... 143
13. ACKNOWLEDGMENTS 147
14. AUTHOR'S NOTE... 148
....148

INTRODUCTION

The "Island of Beauty," Corsica, lures visitors with an attraction that goes beyond simple explanation. It is tucked away like a hidden gem in the cerulean embrace of the Mediterranean Sea. This mysterious island, a rocky treasure off the coast of France, is a place where stories and history converge with the astounding creativity of nature.

Mountains embrace the sky in Corsica, their granite summits covered with tales of legendary warriors. The Mediterranean Sea meets exquisite beaches with smooth, sun-kissed sand here, offering adventure and comfort to those who seek it. The Corsican mentality, proud and robust, weaves its tale through picturesque villages and busy towns in Corsica, which is more than simply a retreat for nature lovers.

You'll come across a world of contrasts as you travel the island: the busy harbor of Ajaccio, the peaceful solitude of Bonifacio, the vivid colors of local markets, and the eternal tranquility of centuries-old towns. It is a location where the perfume of freshly made pastries combines with that of the aromatic Corsican scrubland known as the maquis.

Ancient Genoese towers and strongholds serve as the guardians of time, imprinting Corsica's history into the very fabric of the island. Corsica is still very much alive, celebrating its customs, music, and passionate people despite the ghosts of the past.

We welcome you to discover Corsica's secrets in this book and to trek its challenging paths, enjoy its cuisine, and swim in its azure seas. Every tourist may find a special adventure in Corsica, regardless of whether they value the outdoors, are interested in history, or are just looking for peace and quiet. This magical island is more than just a place to visit; it's an experience just waiting to be lived. Welcome to Corsica, where the stunning scenery and kind locals will enchant your heart and soul.

1. GEOGRAPHICAL OVERVIEW

The "Island of Beauty," Corsica, is a place unto itself where every feature of the terrain tells a story of the passage of time. Rich valleys, meadows, and scenic plateaus beautify its center, while rugged escarpments guard the island's secrets like sentinels. Corsica is an island that defies categorization; it is tucked away in the cerulean cradle of the Mediterranean Sea like a lost gem. With each brushstroke of nature's paintbrush creating a brand-new masterpiece, its geography reads like an artist's portfolio.

The raw, untamed interior of Corsica is dominated by towering, rocky mountains. The patchwork of landscapes that spreads below is watched over by Monte Cinto, the island's highest guardian. The interior of Corsica is a land of grand adventures, with paths winding past immaculate, mirror-like lakes and through old-growth woods. The island's main treasure, the shoreline, however, steals the show. Golden beaches meet the Mediterranean's crystal-clear seas here, while secluded coves speak of delights yet to be uncovered. Cliffs keep watch over these secrets. The coastline of Corsica, which stretches for more than 1,000 kilometers, is a tribute to nature's inventiveness.

The topography of Corsica is a patchwork of various landscapes that caters to the tastes of all tourists. The island is divided into two separate geographic areas: the untamed interior with its mountains and the lovely coastal sections. The wild and untamed interior of Corsica is renowned for its spectacular vistas and abundant fauna. The Corsican Mountains, the island's most recognizable feature, are found in the Corsican heartland.

Greek Mountains
• Monte Cinto: At 2,706 meters (8,878 feet) above sea level, Monte Cinto is Corsica's tallest peak. This strenuous ascent's spectacular vistas are what entice hikers to it.

• GR20 Trail: The GR20 traverses the whole island and is one of Europe's most well-known long-distance hiking paths. It leads walkers through thick forests, across lofty plateaus, and along slender hills.

Natural Reserves
• Parc Naturel Régional de Corse: This regional park, which occupies about 40% of the island, provides outstanding chances for trekking, animal viewing, and wilderness exploration in Corsica.

• Scandola Nature Reserve: This UNESCO World Heritage Site is distinguished by its stunning red cliffs and crystal-clear lakes. A distinctive viewpoint of this unspoiled coastal region is provided by boat trips.

Mountains' Villages
• Corte: Situated in the middle of the mountains, Corte is well-known for having played a crucial role in the

development of Corsican nationalism. Visit its renowned citadel and explore the ancient town.

• Sartène: A gorgeous site with winding alleyways and historic structures, Sartène is a delightful hilltop hamlet with a history stretching back to Roman times.

You'll be engulfed in a symphony of aromas as you go through the maquis, Corsica's beautiful wildness. An island-specific scent, the fragrant combination of wild plants and blooms is an olfactory marvel. The calm lakes on the island, where reflections of the mountains reflect the skies, are where the island's spirit dwells. Nestled in the center of the Restonica Valley, Lake Melu and Lac de Capitello are like twin gems being held in the hands of nature. You may feel the entrancing perfume of wild plants and blooms as you walk through the maquis, Corsica's aromatic scrubland—a symphony of scents that are exclusive to this region. This alluring aroma permeates the air and transports you to the island's breathtaking natural beauty.

The varied geography of Corsica is a haven for those who seek adventure. Daredevils can test their mettle against the uncontrollable elements in its rivers and canyons. Exhilarating sensations may be had in the Tavignano Valley and the Gorges of Restonica, as if nature itself worked to design the ultimate thrill ride. Corsica's immaculate beaches are set against stunning coastal cliffs that the surf has carved. Fine-sand beaches like Plage de Palombaggia and Plage de Saleccia beckon visitors to unwind, while the rocky beauty of the Calanques de Piana reveals nature's skill in crafting stone.

The towns and cities of Corsica are like pearls nestled inside the crown of the island, from the busy harbors of Ajaccio and Bastia to the serene tranquility of Bonifacio's cliffs. The fusion of modernity and antiquity generates a certain appeal that charms tourists.

The topography of Corsica serves as both a foreground and a protagonist in a story of discovery and awe. Every walk through the maquis, every look out at the sea, and every trip through the mountains is a voyage into the heart of a place that wears its beauty on its sleeve and welcomes everyone who is looking for its riches.

HISTORICAL SIGNIFICANCE

Every stone in Corsica, often known as the "Island of History," has a tale to tell, and every road goes somewhere in the past. This island allows you to travel through history's annals like a time machine, making the past feel vividly present.

Imagine yourself on the cobblestone streets of Ajaccio, the famed Napoleon Bonaparte's birthplace. The intensity of a young lad who would grow up to conquer half of Europe is nearly audible in the echo of his footsteps.

More than simply legends from the distant past, Corsica's history is a symbol of tenacity. The Corsican Republic was founded in the 18th century by the island's own Pasquale Paoli. At that time, Corsica was more than simply a pawn on the chessboards of empires; it was a symbol of independence and freedom.

You'll come across historic Genoese turrets as you travel through the Corsican countryside that were constructed centuries ago to fight against pirates and marauders. You'll see prehistoric megalithic ruins where you can almost hear the murmurs of individuals who helped define the history of the island.

History in Corsica is not just about famous people or iconic structures; it also touches on the character of the island nation. The people who live here are more than just locals; they are the heirs of a history of resistance and tenacity. The Corsican identity is a product of many years of struggle, and this energy is still blazing today. In Corsica, history isn't preserved behind glass in a museum; rather, it's there in the rocks under your feet, the villagers' tales, and the air itself. Every time you visit, you have the chance to participate in a timeless story because the island's historical significance acts as an unseen thread tying together the past, present, and future. As a result, as you walk across Corsica, you also move through time.

Imagine yourself in the sleepy town of Corte, which is tucked away in the untamed Corsican highlands. Pasquale Paoli proclaimed Corsican independence here, in the very center of

Corsica, in 1755. History was made right here when a little island asserted its right to self-determination.

The history of Corsica is a tapestry made of strands of resistance and tenacity. As a people who have seen occupation, conflict, and shifting tides of empire, the Corsicans have never given up their identity or longing for freedom.

The magnificent citadels that cling to rocks above the sea are living examples of the Genoese inheritance. You will walk on the same ground as the Genoese conquerors as you explore Calvi's fortress. You may also travel back in time by visiting Bonifacio, whose historic fortifications stare out over the wonderfully blue Mediterranean.

The megalithic ruins of Corsica, like Filitosa, are like windows into the history of the island. You can't help but ponder the life of the prehistoric Corsicans who fashioned these mysterious statues from stone.

The past of Corsica is not some far-off memory; rather, it is an active aspect of the island's present. Corsican food is prepared using recipes that have been handed down through the years. You follow in the footsteps of explorers, revolutionaries, and visionaries as you stroll through the towns' streets.

So, when you travel to Corsica, it's more than simply a vacation—it's a time-traveling trip. Every cobblestone, castle, and Corsican grin is a chapter in a tale of tenacity, freedom, and the steadfast character of an island that has created history in equal measure to how it has been shaped by it. Corsica is more than simply a location on a map; it's a trip through time where the present and past come together to create an experience that will live in your memory forever.

WHY TRAVEL TO CORSICA?

Corsica, sometimes known as the "Island of Beauty," is a location that defies categorization. It is a place that attracts visitors with a magnetic charm and offers a distinctive fusion of natural beauty, historical significance, and dynamic culture. Here are some strong arguments for why you should put Corsica on your bucket list of places to visit.

1. Wild and beautiful landscapes
The topography of Corsica is a display of the craftsmanship of nature. It has breathtaking coastlines, tall mountains, and thick woods. While the dense maquis, a fragrant scrubland, is a paradise for hikers and nature lovers, the island's highest summit, Monte Cinto, encourages explorers to explore its pristine routes.

2. Immaculate Beaches and Clear Waters
The more than 1,000 kilometers of coastline in Corsica are a beach lover's paradise. The island's beaches provide peace and

adventure, with chances for swimming, snorkeling, and watersports in the Mediterranean Sea's crystal-clear waters. They range from golden, sandy coasts to secret coves flanked by towering cliffs.

3. A Trip Through Time
The historical importance of Corsica is a time-travel adventure. From the ancient Greeks and Romans to the Genoese and Corsican rebels, the island has been changed over many centuries by history. Visit historic castles, megalithic ruins, and lovely towns where the ground is alive with history.

4. The Resilience Spirit
The history of Corsica is one of tenacity. Despite being subjected to occupations, wars, and empires, the Corsican people's identity and longing for freedom have not changed. Pasquale Paoli, a rebel who founded the Corsican Republic in the 18th century and became a symbol of self-government and democratic values, was born on the island.

5. Cultural Wealth
Corsica is a veritable treasury of cultural encounters. Immerse yourself in Corsican culture and language, indulge in scrumptious charcuterie and cheeses, and take part in regional celebrations where the spirit and traditions of the island are brought to life through song, dancing, and friendship.

6. Adventure Is Waiting

Corsica has a wide range of activities for those looking for adventure. Explore the island's gorgeous national parks, hike through difficult gorges, and go diving to see marine life and other underwater treasures.

7. Friendly individuals:
The inhabitants of Corsica are renowned for their generous hospitality. You'll experience a real and kind welcome wherever you go, whether you're touring bustling metropolises or far-flung villages. This will make your trip even more unforgettable.

Corsica is more than just a place to go; it's an entire journey that immerses you in the region's history, culture, and natural beauty. Every step is an adventure, every view is a postcard, and every moment is an opportunity to form enduring memories on the island thanks to its untainted beauty, steadfast history, and the kindness of its people. When you travel to Corsica, you will experience a voyage that will captivate your heart and soul and instill a lasting passion for the "Island of Beauty."

2. PLANNING YOUR TRIP

BEST TIME TO VISIT

The Mediterranean island of Corsica is a treasure that draws tourists with its fascinating history, varied scenery, and lively culture. Corsica offers it all, whether you're looking for sandy beaches, untamed mountains, or quaint coastal villages. But when is the ideal time to travel to this magical place? Your tastes will determine the response, as each season on the island offers a different experience.

Let us guide you through the Corsican calendar to help you choose the best time to organize your trip to Corsica, from the vivacious bloom of spring to the peaceful stillness of winter. We have options for everyone, whether you enjoy the sun, hiking, history, or local festivals.

April to May: Springtime Bliss

Corsica is gently awakened from its winter slumber by the arrival of spring. The environment is overflowing with beautiful colors of green throughout this season, which is one of rejuvenation. Spring can be the ideal season to go if you enjoy being outside, hiking, or preferring warmer weather.

1. Climate and Weather:
• Temperatures: The spring season in Corsica is suitable for outdoor activities, with typical daily temperatures ranging from 15°C (59°F) in April to 21°C (70°F) in May.
• Rainfall: While there may still be sporadic showers, the total amount of precipitation is lower than it was during the rainier winter months.

• Setting: The island's luxuriant vegetation and blooming flowers provide a beautiful setting for exploring.

2. Highlights and Activities:
• Hiking: Spring is the ideal time to go hiking since the weather is nice and there are fewer people on the trails. Examine the well-known GR20 track or select slower treks in Corsica's national parks.
Wildflowers: Take in the beautiful hues of the island's wildflowers, which are currently in full bloom.
• Pre-Season Calm: Take advantage of the island's attractions when there are fewer visitors, which makes it a great time for relaxing exploration.

3. Local Holidays:
• Fête du Travu (Chestnut Celebration): At this exciting celebration, savor the gastronomic delicacies of the island, including traditional chestnut recipes.
• Fiera di u Vinu (Wine Fair): If you enjoy wine, you should check out this celebration of Corsican wine, which offers tasting possibilities.

(June through August) Summer Bliss:

The busiest travel season in Corsica is summer, when the island comes to life. It's the ideal season for sunbathers and beach lovers with its sun-drenched beaches, mild oceans, and bustling coastal towns.

1. Climate and Weather

• Temperatures: In the summer, Corsica has temperatures that range from approximately 25°C (77°F) in June to as high as 30°C (86°F) in July and August.
• Sunlight: Clear skies and plenty of sunlight are to be expected, making this the perfect time for beach activities.

2. Highlights and Activities
• Beaches: Corsica's magnificent coastline, which has well-known locations like Palombaggia and Saleccia, is ideal for swimming, watersports, and sunbathing.
• Water Activities: Take part in sailing, scuba diving, and snorkeling in the pristine seas.
• Festive Atmosphere: The vibrant nightlife, lively atmospheres, and waterfront restaurants bring coastal communities to life.

3. Local Holidays
• Calvi on the Rocks: This well-known music event plays electronic and independent music, resulting in a distinctive beach party ambiance.
• Porto Latino: In Saint-Florent, celebrate the island's rich cultural history with music, dancing, and fireworks.

Fall's Enchantment (September through October):

Corsica has a new allure when the summer gradually gives way to the fall. This is a great time to visit the island if you like a more sedate pace of exploration because it is less busy and the weather is still lovely.

1. Climate and Weather

• Temperatures: There is a suitable atmosphere for outdoor activities, with average temperatures ranging from 26°C (79°F) in September to about 21°C (70°F) in October.
• Fewer People: Take advantage of popular sights without the summer rush.

2. Highlights and Activities
• Hiking and the outdoors: Take advantage of the pleasant weather to go on hikes, explore the verdant forests, and find secret coves.
• Grape harvest season: Corsica's vineyards come alive at this time, providing an opportunity to enjoy the region's wines.
• Cultural exploration: explore museums and historical places away from the summertime crowd.

3. Local Holidays
• Foire de l'Amandier (Almond Fair): This celebration of Corsican almonds features delectable sweets made with almonds.
Car aficionados may watch the Corsican leg of the World Rally Championship at the Rallye Tour de Corse.

Serenity of Winter (November through March):

In Corsica, winter is a time of seclusion and tranquility. The island's tranquil charm, moderate environment, and historical attractions can be the perfect draw for your visit if you like a relaxing holiday.

1. Climate and Weather

• Temperatures: Winter is a mild season for exploration, with daytime highs of 10°C (50°F) and nighttime lows of 5°C (41°F).
Quieter Ambience

Visit the island's historical and cultural landmarks when there aren't many people around.

2. Highlights and Activities
• Historical Exploration: Visit historic fortifications, megalithic ruins, and quaint towns to learn more about Corsica's extensive past.
• Cultural Immersion: Participate in Corsican customs and interact with people in a more personal environment.
• Nature Walks: While the winter is not the ideal time to go swimming, it does provide peaceful country walks.

3. Local Holidays
• Christmas Markets: Visit regional Christmas markets to take part in Corsican holiday customs and browse for one-of-a-kind presents.
• Carnival: Take part in the vibrant and exuberant Carnival celebrations to honor Corsican culture.

In conclusion, Corsica is a year-round paradise that provides activities for all tastes and interests. Every season in Corsica has something to offer, whether you're a sun worshiper, an outdoor explorer, a history buff, or a cultural aficionado. Find your ideal window of opportunity to visit this gem of the Mediterranean and start your adventure through its splendor, rich past, and active present.

ENTRY AND VISA REQUIREMENTS

Your nationality and vacation plans will determine whether you need a visa and how to enter Corsica. Since Corsica is a part of France, it abides by the country's and the Schengen Area's visa and entrance requirements.

Members of the Schengen Area
As a part of France, Corsica belongs to the Schengen Area, a collection of European nations that have done away with passport checks and other forms of border control at their shared borders. When traveling to Corsica, you often only have to go through a passport check once—either when entering or exiting the Schengen Zone.

1. Visa prerequisites
• Citizens of the European Union (EU) and the European Economic Area (EEA): You do not require a visa to enter Corsica if you are a citizen of an EU or EEA nation. As long as your passport or national ID card is current, you may stay for an indefinite amount of time.

• Non-EU/EEA Citizens: Your admission criteria may change if you are not a citizen of an EU or EEA nation. In general, a Schengen visa may be required for entry into Corsica. Depending on why you are visiting, you may need a tourist, business, or another sort of visa. Before your journey, you should apply for this visa at the French embassy or consulate in your country.

2. Validity of passport:
Your passport must be valid for at least three months after the day you want to leave Corsica. Make sure your passport has blank pages so you can get any essential stamps at the border and upon leaving.

3. Duration of stay:
Within a 180-day window, visitors from nations without visa requirements are permitted a 90-day stay in Corsica and the Schengen region. You might need to apply for a certain visa if you want to remain longer or for a different reason.

4. Return Ticket and Money:
Border officials may want a return ticket or confirmation that you have enough money to cover your stay.

5. Travel Protection:
Since Corsica has its own healthcare system, it is recommended to obtain travel insurance that covers accidents and illnesses. Comprehensive travel insurance might be useful in an emergency.

6. Regulations for Customs:
Become familiar with Corsica's customs laws and the list of products you are permitted to carry into the country duty-free. The use of substances like alcohol and cigarettes is restricted.

7. Border control and security:

When entering Corsica, be prepared for usual security and border inspections as the island is a part of France and is subject to standard French security processes.

Please be aware that admission requirements sometimes vary, so it's important to get the most recent information from reliable sources before your travel to Corsica, such as the French embassy or consulate in your home country or the official French government website. Additionally, take into account seeking particular guidance from the embassy or consulate based on your country of citizenship and travel objectives.

BUDGETING AND CURRENCY

The "Island of Beauty" in the Mediterranean, Corsica, promises visitors a distinctive fusion of environment, history, and culture. Understanding the local currency and wise planning will improve your experience and guarantee smooth travel as you prepare for your Corsican excursion.

Corsican currency
The Euro (EUR) is the official unit of currency for Corsica, which is a part of France. The European Union (EU) uses the euro as its official currency, making it the second-most popular reserve currency in the world. As a result of this homogeneity, visiting Corsica from an EU country is simple because they may use the same currency. The euro is a well-known and commonly used currency on the island.

Here are some useful pointers to aid with your financial planning:

Consider exchanging some money at your neighborhood bank or currency exchange provider before starting your trip to Corsica. You'll arrive with cash in hand if you do it that way. You may locate ATMs in major cities and towns in Corsica because the country has a strong financial infrastructure. Hotels, restaurants, and retail establishments frequently accept credit cards like Visa and MasterCard. However, it's a good idea to have some cash on hand, especially in rural regions, for smaller, neighborhood shops.

Consider creating a daily budget to efficiently manage your spending. Your travel style will determine how much money you need. Your daily spending will be different from someone who favors local restaurants, for instance, if you want to dine at expensive restaurants.

Your budget includes a sizable amount for lodging. Corsica has a variety of lodging choices, from opulent resorts to inexpensive hostels and campers. It is best to plan ahead and reserve your lodgings, especially during the busiest travel season.

In addition to charcuterie, cheese, and regional wines, Corsica is renowned for its delectable gastronomy. By eating at neighborhood eateries and experimenting with traditional foods, you may reduce your food bills. If you choose high-end eating, be aware that the expenses will be greater.

Your travel expenditures may differ depending on your itinerary. If you wish to travel to the island's more distant sections, renting a car might be practical but pricey. Buses and trains are examples of public transportation that is more cost-effective. From hiking and water sports to seeing ancient sites, Corsica has a wide range of activities to choose from. Make a budgetary plan for these experiences and schedule your activities in advance. Local crafts, wines, and delicacies from Corsica are just a few of the island's distinctive goods. Set aside money for souvenirs and shopping.

Always keep some cash on hand to cover unanticipated costs like last-minute changes to your vacation plans or medical problems. Use currency conversion tools to help you monitor your spending in real-time and, if necessary, translate prices into your local currency.

Effective Corsican budgeting
Despite being famed for its natural beauty and adventure, Corsica is accessible to travelers of all financial levels. Here is some practical financial advice to help you make the most of your trip to Corsica, whether you're a luxury tourist, a midrange adventurer, or a thrifty backpacker:

1. Accommodation:
 Luxury Travelers: If you're looking for luxury, Corsica has a variety of upmarket alternatives, including boutique hotels and beach resorts. Set aside a sizable amount of your cash for luxurious lodging.
Mid-Range Travelers: Travelers on a mid-range budget may have relaxing stays in quaint guesthouses, villas, and

three-star hotels. For the best deals, do your homework and make your reservations in advance because prices vary based on the area and the season.

Backpackers on a tight budget: The island is dotted with hostels, campsites, and inexpensive guesthouses. With so many campsites accessible, camping in Corsica is a particularly economical choice.

2. Dining:

Luxury Travelers: Indulging in Corsican specialties at fine dining establishments may be a delightful experience. Budget some of your money for upscale meals and wine sampling.

Mid-Range Explorers: Enjoy Corsican charcuterie, cheeses, and shellfish at affordable costs in restaurants and cafés that serve local cuisine.

Backpackers on a tight budget should choose self-catering or low-cost local restaurants to reduce their food expenses. For those on a tight budget, local markets and fresh vegetables are excellent choices.

3. Adventures and Activities:

Luxury tourists: When it comes to activities, the options are virtually endless for luxury tourists. Think about escorted tours, VIP excursions, and private boat cruises.

Mid-Range Explorers: Take part in a variety of low-cost and high-cost activities, such as hiking, beachcombing, and visiting historical sites. Corsica has a wide range of affordable natural and cultural attractions.

Backpackers on a tight budget may enjoy Corsica's scenic surroundings by swimming, hiking, and exploring for very little money. The finest activities on the island, including trekking in national parks, are frequently cost-free.

4. Transportation:
Luxury guests: private transfers, automobile rentals, and first-rate transportation services are all available for the convenience of luxury guests.
Mid-Range Explorers: Corsica may be explored affordably via public transportation, such as trains, buses, and local ferries. For those who want to go off the main route, renting a car is another choice.
Budget planes, shared transportation, and cycling may be the most cost-effective alternatives for backpackers to get around the island.

5. Supplemental Charges:
Luxury Travelers: Set aside money for one-of-a-kind experiences like boat rentals, spa visits, and private excursions.
Mid-Range Explorers: Budget for supplemental costs, including entrance fees to natural parks, historic site admission fees, and minor memento purchases.
Budget-conscious travelers should keep a reserve set aside for unforeseen costs, emergencies, and pleasant surprises.

Local Savings Advice:

• Local Markets: Browse Corsica's thriving markets for local goods, fresh vegetables, and handcrafted items. Although it is uncommon, you may obtain high-quality goods for fair costs.

• Picnics: Indulge in a leisurely picnic with regional foods at one of Corsica's picturesque locations. It's an affordable way to experience the island's tastes and its scenic splendor.

• Take advantage of the island's breathtaking natural attractions, including hiking trails, beaches, and historic monuments, which sometimes have low or free admission costs.

• Travel Off-Peak: To take advantage of reduced pricing and fewer crowds, consider visiting Corsica in the shoulder seasons (spring and fall).

In the end, how much money you spend on your Corsican vacation depends on your choices and travel style. Corsica offers plenty to offer every kind of traveler, whether they choose to splurge on opulent experiences, choose midrange comforts, or embrace budget-friendly travel. The finest of Corsica may be enjoyed without breaking the bank if your spending is wisely planned, making your trip to the Mediterranean an unforgettable vacation.

SPEAKING AND INTERACTION

The history of the island has had an impact on Corsica's language and communication, with a mix of French and Corsican (an Italian-influenced dialect) being the two main languages used. An outline of Corsican communication and language is provided below:

1. Language of Corsica:
Corsican, often known as Corsu in Corsican, is an indigenous language heavily influenced by Italian. It is valued in the island's culture and acknowledged as a regional tongue. Despite the fact that not everyone in Corsica speaks the language, many of them are proud of their linguistic history and can speak and comprehend it to varied degrees. Corsican is more often used in casual discourse in some areas.

2. English Language:
The official language of Corsica is French, which is widely spoken and understood across the whole island. It is the language used in business, education, and administration. French speakers won't have any problem getting by in Corsica. Additionally, the majority of tourist services are offered in French.

3. Languages Other Than English:
Despite the fact that English is not as widely spoken as French, you will discover that many people in the tourism sector, especially in popular tourist destinations, can speak the language. Learning a few fundamental French words may make traveling easier, especially in less-visited areas.

4. Language aspects to consider
• Regional Variations: There are regional differences in Corsican dialects. As you go over the island, don't be shocked

if you hear different accents or idioms because Corsican has several dialects, each with small grammatical variances.

• Cultural Significance: Corsicans can be quite appreciative of anyone who speaks a little Corsican or who shows an interest in the native tongue. It allows you to engage with the island's history and culture.

5. Interacting with the Community:
Corsicans are often cordial and welcoming, and they like it when visitors try to speak a little French or Corsican. Everybody appreciates a kind "hello" (bonjour or bonghjornu in Corsican) and a "thank you" (merci or grazie in Corsican).

Both Corsican and French menus are available at cafés and restaurants. Never be afraid to ask the waitress for further information on a dish if you have any questions. It's helpful to know a few basic French phrases or use translation software to help you when asking for directions or information.

The variety of languages spoken in Corsica reflects the island's long history and diverse culture. Although French is the main language used for communication, understanding Corsican might help you feel more connected to Corsica's distinctive culture. Corsican is an essential component of the island's character

3. GETTING TO CORSICA

BY AIR (Flying to Corsica)

Getting to Corsica by flight is a practical and regular way to visit the island. Corsica has many airports that serve different regions, making it accessible from various European cities. Here's a guide on how to get to Corsica by flight and an overview of the major airports on the island:

1. International Airports: Corsica has many international airports, the largest ones being Ajaccio-Napoléon Bonaparte Airport (AJA) and Bastia-Poretta Airport (BIA).

2. Regional Airports: Other airports, such as Calvi-Sainte-Catherine Airport (CLY), Figari-Sud Corse Airport (FSC), and Ile-Rousse-Balagne Airport (LFK), are regional airports that cater to certain sections of the island.

• Flights: You may get direct flights to Corsica from numerous European locations, especially during the high tourist season. These flights are typically operated by major European airlines and low-cost carriers.

3. Major Airports in Corsica:
• Ajaccio-Napoléon Bonaparte Airport (AJA): Located near Ajaccio on the western coast of Corsica, this airport is the largest on the island. It serves both domestic and international aircraft, giving it a handy entrance point.
• Bastia-Poretta Airport (BIA): Situated in the northeastern portion of Corsica near Bastia, this airport handles local and international flights. It's a significant entrance for travelers visiting the northern sections of the island.
• Calvi-Sainte-Catherine Airport (CLY): Located in Calvi in the northwest, this airport primarily serves the Balagne region and is a popular alternative for people exploring that area.

• Figari-Sud Corse Airport (FSC): Situated in the southern portion of Corsica, near Porto-Vecchio and Bonifacio, this airport offers a gateway to the southern region of the island.
• Île-Rousse-Balagne Airport (LFK): Serving the Balagne region in the northwest, this airport offers a smaller choice for travelers traveling to that specific area.

4. Seasonal Variations: Flight availability and frequency might vary based on the time of year. The summer months (June to August) feature more travel possibilities due to the busy tourist season, whereas in the shoulder seasons (spring and fall), there may be fewer flights available.

5. Transportation from Airports: Corsica's airports are well connected to the island's road network. You can hire a vehicle, employ shuttle services, or use cabs to reach your ultimate location. Public transit alternatives like buses are also available.

6. Travel Tips
• Book in Advance: Especially during the high summer season, it's advised to book your flights well in advance to obtain the greatest costs and availability.

• Arrival Time: Arriving during the daylight helps you better manage transportation choices and get comfortable in your hotel.

• Check Local Transportation: Before your journey, explore local transportation choices from the airport to your ultimate destination, since they might differ by location.

Getting to Corsica by air is an easy affair, given its well-connected airports and the availability of flights from many European towns. Once you arrive, you may explore the different landscapes and rich culture of this wonderful Mediterranean island.

GETTING TO CORSICA BY SEA

Getting to Corsica by boat is a popular and picturesque way to approach the island, giving a unique view of its magnificent coastline. Corsica is well-connected by ferry services from mainland France and Italy, making the island accessible for vacationers with or without automobiles. Here's a guide on how to get to Corsica by sea:

1. Major Ports in Corsica

• Bastia: Located in the northeastern portion of the island, Bastia is one of Corsica's principal ferry ports. Ferries from Italy, mainland France, and other Mediterranean locations regularly arrive in BaBastia.

• Ajaccio: In the west, Ajaccio serves as another main ferry port in Corsica. It offers connectivity to the French mainland and sometimes Italy.

• Calvi: Situated in the northwest, Calvi is a minor port that provides ferry routes, particularly from the French mainland.

• Ile-Rousse: This port in the Balagne area in the northwest provides ferry services, particularly to the French mainland.

• Propriano: Found in the southern section of Corsica, Propriano has ferry connections, including runs to Toulon on the French mainland.

2. Ferry Routes

• France to Corsica: There are various ferry routes linking Corsica to the French mainland. The most popular French departure ports were Marseille, Nice, Toulon, and Portoferraio (Elba). The arriving ports of Corsica are notably Bastia, Ajaccio, Calvi, Ile-Rousse, and Propriano.

• Italy to Corsica: From Italy, ferries link to Corsica from numerous ports, including Livorno, Genoa, Savona, and Civitavecchia. The principal ports arriving in Corsica are Bastia and Ajaccio.

• Sardinia to Corsica: Some ferry lines link Corsica to Sardinia, including departures from ports such as Santa Teresa Gallura and Bonifacio.

3. Ferry Operators: Several ferry companies provide services to Corsica, giving a range of alternatives in terms of comfort, speed, and car transportation. Popular operators include Corsica Ferries, Moby Lines, La Méridionale, and more.

4. Booking Tickets: It's best to reserve your boat tickets in advance, especially during the high summer season. You may order tickets through the websites of ferry companies, travel agencies, or at the ports.

5. Travel Time: The duration of the ferry travel might vary based on the departure and arrival ports, the vessel's speed, and the route. Generally, crossings from mainland France to Corsica take roughly 4-6 hours, whereas crossings from Italy might take longer, depending on the point of departure.

6. Vehicle Transportation: If you want to transport a vehicle, whether it's a car, RV, or motorcycle, you should arrange a spot for it on the boat in advance. Vehicle transportation expenses might vary based on the size of the vehicle.

7. Facilities Onboard: Most ferries are provided with facilities including restaurants, bars, accommodations for longer voyages, and deck spaces for enjoying the sea views.

Traveling to Corsica by boat gives a unique and attractive approach to the island. As you reach the shore, you'll be met with the island's steep cliffs, gorgeous beaches, and lush surroundings. Whether you're arriving from mainland France, Italy, or Sardinia, the ferry ride itself becomes a fascinating aspect of your Corsican vacation.

TRANSPORTATION WITHIN CORSICA

Transportation inside Corsica is rather convenient, allowing you to see the island's different landscapes, from its attractive coastal cities to its mountainous interiors. Here are the primary types of transportation throughout Corsica:

1. Rental cars

Renting a car is one of the most popular and flexible ways to see Corsica. You may hire a car at major airports and cities on the island. Having your own vehicle helps you explore remote areas and picturesque communities, especially in hilly regions. However, it's advised to book your rental car in advance during the busy summer months.

2. Public buses

Corsica has a network of public buses run by numerous firms. The buses link major towns and cities on the island and offer a cheap way to move around. Bus schedules might change; therefore, it's vital to verify the timetables and routes in advance. Keep in mind that certain routes may have restricted operation during the off-peak season.

3. Trains

Corsica has a unique rail system known as "Chemins de fer de la Corse" (CFC). While the rail network is small compared to other transit alternatives, it offers a pleasant way to travel between cities and appreciate the island's gorgeous surroundings. The railroad connects Bastia with Ajaccio, going through Corte and other cities.

4. Taxis

Taxis are accessible in major cities and villages, offering on-demand transportation. They might be a useful choice for short trips inside metropolitan regions. You may discover taxi ranks near transit hubs and city centers.

5. Ferries and Boats

Given Corsica's coastline position, ferries and boats are employed for inter-island transit. For example, you may take boats to visit the magnificent Scandola Nature Reserve and the adjacent island of Elba. There are also boat rides offered for lovely coastline excursions.

6. Cycling

Corsica provides fantastic chances for cycling enthusiasts. Many routes, especially in the interior, are well-suited for cycling. You may bring your bicycle or hire one on the island. There are cycling paths like the "Veilles Pédagogiques" for people interested in discovering Corsica on two wheels.

7. Walking and Hiking

Corsica features various hiking paths, with the most notable being the GR20. Hiking allows you to immerse yourself in the island's natural splendor. Be cautious, check the trail conditions, and select trips that meet your ability level.

8. Car Rentals and Scooters

If you don't want to hire a car for your whole stay, you might consider renting scooters or motorbikes for shorter outings. This might be an exciting way to explore the island's twisting coastline roads.

9. Shared Transportation and Ride-Sharing
Some shared transportation services, such as BlaBlaCar, are available in Corsica. These services can be a cost-effective and eco-friendly way to travel between cities.

While transportation choices in Corsica are typically dependable, the availability of some services may vary based on the season and the exact place you are visiting. When organizing your transportation inside Corsica, it's a good idea to check timetables, book in advance when necessary, and consider your itinerary to make the most of your visit to the "Island of Beauty."

4. CORSICAN REGIONS AND CITIES

AJACCIO: The Corsican Capital and Napoleon's Birthplace

Ajaccio, the capital of Corsica, is a lovely coastal city tucked along the western beaches of the island that mixes history, culture, and natural beauty. It's most notable for being the birthplace of Napoleon Bonaparte. Visitors may explore the city's historic and cultural monuments, as well as enjoy its gorgeous beaches and waterfront promenades.

With its historic significance as the birthplace of Napoleon Bonaparte and its gorgeous Mediterranean settings, Ajaccio provides a vivid introduction to Corsican culture and history.

Ajaccio's Culture and Language

Ajaccio is profoundly steeped in Corsican culture, a unique combination of Italian and French elements. This unique cultural combination is an intrinsic part of daily life, with strong family relationships and a profound connection to the island's past.

While French serves as the official language, you'll commonly hear Corsican (Corsu) spoken by the inhabitants. Corsican is more than just a language; it's a sign of Corsican identity.

Street signs in Ajaccio illustrate this language diversity, exhibiting both French and Corsican names.

Historical landmarks, museums, and must-see attractions

- Maison Bonaparte: A must-visit destination is Maison Bonaparte, the family house where Napoleon was born in 1769. Maison Bonaparte is a well-conserved ancient house that has been turned into a museum. It gives an intimate glimpse into the life and family of the renowned Corsican, allowing visitors to understand the lives of this important character.

- The Cathedral of Ajaccio: This 16th-century Baroque cathedral is an architectural jewel and an important religious destination. It is a masterpiece of Corsican Baroque architecture. The magnificent construction it features includes its beautiful frescoes and stained glass windows while enjoying the tranquil environment.

- Fesch Museum: The Fesch Museum, created by Cardinal Joseph Fesch, Napoleon's uncle, includes an excellent and vast collection of European paintings (Italian and Corsican art), affording an insight into the island's cultural legacy.

- Citadel of Ajaccio: The citadel overlooks the city and gives panoramic views of the bay. It's a fantastic area for a leisurely stroll and to explore the local history museum.

- Sanguinaires Islands: A short boat journey from Ajaccio brings you to the Sanguinaires Islands, noted for their beautiful crimson sunsets. Discover the rough terrain, take a trek, and marvel at the antique lighthouse.

- City Beaches: Ajaccio features numerous magnificent beaches, including Plage de Marinella and Plage de la Stagnola, where you can relax and enjoy the Mediterranean sun. We also have swimming beaches such as St. François Beach, one of Ajaccio's most popular beaches, located near the city center. It's great for sunbathing and swimming, and Trottel Beach lures travelers for sun-soaked leisure and exhilarating swims in the Mediterranean Seas.

Festive Moments and Celebrations
- Napoleon Bonaparte Celebrations: On August 15th, Ajaccio comes alive with celebrations and reenactments in honor of its most famous resident, Napoleon Bonaparte. Immerse yourself in the period of the Corsican emperor with parades, historical reenactments, and cultural activities.

- Corsican Carnival (A Fiera di Castagna): Experience the vivid atmosphere of the Corsican Carnival, held in Ajaccio and other cities around the island. Revel in bright parades, traditional costumes, and exciting street entertainment.

Culinary Delights

Ajaccio provides a choice of eating experiences, from seafood restaurants on the port to lovely cafés. Sample Corsican specialties include brocciu cheese, wild boar, and seafood delicacies.

Corsican cuisine is recognized for its superb ingredients and wonderful tastes. Taste beautiful cheeses like brocciu, relish the rich charcuterie selections of lonzu and figatellu, and delight in fresh seafood taken from the adjacent Mediterranean shores.

- Local Delicacies: Don't miss out on renowned Corsican cuisine, such as wild boar stew (civet de sanglier) and Corsican pizza (pizza corsa), topped with delectable combinations of local ingredients.

Getting Around
- Strolling the Streets: Ajaccio is a tiny city where much may be explored on foot. The city's ancient streets give one an opportunity to immerse oneself in its distinctive atmosphere.

- Public Transport: Local buses provide a handy method of touring both the city and its surrounding areas. They allow quick access to various attractions and picturesque areas.

- Automobile Rentals: For those keen to go farther afield, automobile rentals are readily accessible in Ajaccio. This choice allows you to experience the different landscapes and picturesque villages that Corsica has to offer.

Accommodation Options
- Elegant Waterfront Hotels: Ajaccio provides a range of magnificent waterfront hotels with spectacular sea views and top-notch services. Hotel Les Mouettes, positioned on the seashore, provides a unique blend of comfort and elegance.

- Central Hotels: Hotels like Hotel Marengo and Hotel San Carlu give quick access to the city's attractions and the colorful ambience of Ajaccio's streets.

- Vacation Rentals: If you prefer a more domestic setting, you'll discover a choice of vacation rentals and apartments dotted across the city. These choices offer greater room and cooking amenities for enhanced convenience.

- Hostels and Guesthouses: Budget-conscious tourists will welcome the availability of hostels and guesthouses, which offer inexpensive prices and the opportunity to interact with fellow explorers.

Ajaccio's rich cultural heritage, excellent food, interesting history, and breathtaking beauty lure tourists from all walks of life. Whether you're meandering through its medieval alleyways, relishing the cuisines of Corsica, or immersing yourself in its vivid festivals, Ajaccio gives a genuinely immersive Corsican experience.

BASTIA

Bastia, another attractive city in Corsica, is known for its rich history, vibrant culture, stunning beaches, and unique attractions. As the second-largest city in Corsica, it serves as a tribute to the island's rich and diversified legacy. Nestled in the northeast, this seaside city features a unique combination of Italian and French influences, providing tourists with an opportunity to immerse themselves in the unique Corsican way of life. From its charming ancient town to the vibrant harbor area, Bastia contains numerous gems waiting to be explored. Bastia's closeness to Cap Corse, a mountainous peninsula, offers options for outdoor pursuits like trekking and exploring gorgeous coastline pathways.

Bastia's Culture and Language
Corsican culture is profoundly interwoven into the fabric of Bastia. The city shows the island's distinctive combination of Mediterranean, Italian, and French influences.

While French is the official language, Corsican (Corsu) is also widely spoken and maintains cultural significance. Street signs and businesses typically feature both languages, underscoring the island's linguistic duality.

Historical landmarks, museums, and must-see attractions
Bastia is more than simply a city; it's a living witness to Corsica's stormy history. Its origins stretch back to the Genoese era, when the Genoese Republic constructed a fortification here. Over time, Bastia grew into a prosperous

port city, with the Old Port (Vieux Port) providing a continual reminder of its nautical legacy.

- The Old Port: This lively waterfront has experienced centuries of commerce and maritime history. Stroll around the quays and grab a coffee at one of the wonderful waterfront cafés. Watch the boats bobbing in the blue seas as you take in the serene environment.

- Citadel of Bastia: This medieval stronghold overlooks the city and affords spectacular views of the shore. Explore its historic walls and meander around the old town streets.

- Museum of Corsica: Housed at the Palais des Gouverneurs, this museum gives insights into Corsica's history, culture, and art. It's a terrific spot to explore further into the island's background.

- Saint-Jean-Baptiste Church: A stunning Baroque church located in the center of Bastia, it's famed for its exquisite stucco decorations and gorgeous altar. It is a prominent religious place and an architectural wonder.

- Terra Vecchia: This picturesque old town district is a tangle of small lanes and antique buildings. It's a great spot for leisurely hikes and uncovering hidden gems.

Festive Moments and Celebrations

Bastia is a city that knows how to rejoice. Be careful to match your visit with one of the city's colorful events. Bastia is a hotspot for cultural events. The city organizes a multitude of events, concerts, and exhibitions that promote Corsican traditions and modern art. The Place Saint-Nicolas is typically at the core of these cultural meetings.

- Bastia Music Festival: This yearly event highlights classical and contemporary music and brings together performers from throughout the world. Enjoy concerts in various places across the city.

- Feast of Saint John the Baptist: Celebrated on June 24th, this celebration is a boisterous occasion replete with processions, music, and dancing. It's a genuine flavor of Corsican customs.

Culinary Delight
Bastia is a gourmet pleasure for food connoisseurs. Corsican cuisine is recognized for its outstanding ingredients and exquisite tastes.

- Fish: Given its seaside position, Bastia provides a profusion of fresh fish. Savor the catch of the day at one of the numerous eateries along the waterfront. Try the famed "bouillabaisse corse," a Corsican spin on the classic fish stew.

- Local Specialties: Sample local dishes like "civet de sanglier" (wild boar stew) and "fiadone," a delectable Corsican cheesecake. The "coppa" and "lonzu" charcuterie are must-try products for individuals who like savory cured meats.

The lonzu originates from the pig's tenderloins. The lonzu is salted according to the traditional procedure. It is then seasoned with a blend of wine and spices. Lonzu is mildly smoked before being fermented in a cellar for many months. Lonzu is produced from filet, which explains why it is a lean chunk.

Getting Around

Bastia boasts a well-connected transit network, giving it a handy base for exploring Corsica.

- Port of Bastia: The city's port is a significant gateway for passengers arriving by ferry from mainland France and Italy. It's a fantastic starting place for visiting other Corsican destinations.

- Train Station: Bastia's train station has rail links to other Corsican cities, making it a good center for visitors looking to explore more of the island's different areas.

- Walking: Bastia's tiny size makes it a perfect destination for leisurely hikes. The town's old streets are a maze of hidden gems waiting to be unearthed.

- Bicycles: Many guests opt for bicycles to explore the town and neighboring trails, giving a leisurely and eco-friendly approach to enjoying the seaside and inland splendor.

- Car Rentals: If you prefer to journey farther into the magnificent Corsican countryside, car rentals are widely accessible, allowing you to explore the island's different areas.

Accommodation options

Bastia provides a range of hotel alternatives to suit different budgets and interests.

- Hotels: From exquisite waterfront hotels with sea views to strategically situated boutique alternatives, you'll discover a selection of pleasant places to stay.

- Apartments and Vacation Rentals: If you want a more domestic ambiance, try renting a vacation apartment in the city.

- Hostels and Guesthouses: Budget travelers can select among hostels and guesthouses, giving reasonable prices and possibilities to interact with fellow travelers.

Bastia's historical significance, unique combination of ethnicities, and gastronomic delights make it a hidden jewel in Corsica. Whether you're walking its old alleys, eating local food, or immersing yourself in its colorful festivals, Bastia provides a one-of-a-kind Corsican experience. It's a city that unveils its mesmerizing appeal one discovery at a time.

CALVI

Calvi, in the northern Balagne area, is a picture-perfect coastal town famed for its magnificent beaches, ancient monuments, and dynamic cultural scene. Calvi, a jewel in the crown of Corsica, is a town that mixes history, natural beauty, and a dynamic environment into a beautiful tapestry of travel experiences.

Calvi's Culture and Language
Calvi pulses with a unique combination of Mediterranean and Corsican culture, providing a compelling atmosphere for visitors.

While French is the official language, Corsican (Corsu) is spoken by many people and is a tribute to Corsica's strong cultural identity.

Historical landmarks, museums, and must-see attractions
The center of Calvi is its medieval fortress, located impressively on a rocky peninsula overlooking the turquoise seas of the Mediterranean. This majestic stronghold gives a look into the town's rich past.

- Citadel of Calvi: Explore the meandering lanes and lovely squares within the citadel's walls. The old Genoese architecture takes you back in time, while the panoramic views of the town and the sea create a timeless background for your tour.

Calvi's coastal position provides it with some of the most stunning beaches in Corsica. The town's beautiful coastlines are noted for their breathtaking vistas and enticing waves.

- Calvi Beach: The town's eponymous beach is a crescent of soft sand and beautiful waves. It's an excellent area for sunbathing, swimming, and water sports. The neighboring promenade offers a profusion of restaurants, cafés, and stores, providing a bustling scene.

- Arinella Beach: For those wanting a calmer and more peaceful beach experience, Arinella Beach is a hidden gem. Nestled between the rocks, it provides an exquisite backdrop for leisure.

Festive Moments and Celebrations

Calvi comes alive during its festive events, giving a peek into Corsican traditions and an opportunity to rejoice with the people.

- Cultural Activities: The town organizes different cultural events, concerts, and exhibitions throughout the year. The Calvi Jazz Festival, held every summer, gathers world-class artists and lovers from all over the world.

- Calvi on the Rocks: An annual electronic music festival held in July, Calvi on the Rocks transforms the town into a bustling party with renowned DJs and seaside events.

- Fête de Sainte Marie: This traditional event, celebrated in mid-August, comprises religious processions, folk music, and a bustling local fair.

Culinary Delight
Corsican cuisine takes center stage in Calvi, providing a feast for the senses. The town's restaurants and cafés exhibit the island's rich gastronomic tradition.

- Fish Extravaganza: As a seaside town, Calvi has an abundance of fresh fish. Savor exquisite prawns, lobster, and sea urchins harvested from the adjacent Mediterranean seas.

- Corsican Delicacies: Indulge in Corsican delicacies like "civet de sanglier" (wild boar stew), "brocciu" (Corsican cheese), and charcuterie treats such as "lonzu" and "figatellu."

Getting Around
Calvi provides a choice of transportation alternatives to explore the town and its surroundings.

- Walking: Calvi's tiny size makes it a perfect destination for leisurely hikes. The town's old streets are a maze of hidden gems waiting to be unearthed.

- Bicycles: Many guests opt for bicycles to explore the town and neighboring trails, giving a leisurely and eco-friendly approach to enjoying the seaside and inland splendor.

- Car Rentals: If you prefer to journey farther into the magnificent Corsican countryside, car rentals are widely accessible, allowing you to explore the island's different areas.

Accommodation options

Calvi has a selection of housing alternatives to suit varied preferences and budgets.

- Hotels: Choose from magnificent seaside hotels, boutique motels, and lovely family-run facilities. Some popular choices are Hotel Revellata, Hotel Mariana, and Hotel Corsica.

- Vacation Rentals: If you want a more domestic setting, try renting a vacation apartment, which gives you the comfort of your own room and cooking amenities.

- Hostels and Guesthouses: Budget-conscious tourists will discover hostels and guesthouses that offer inexpensive prices and the opportunity to socialize with fellow explorers.

Calvi, with its interesting history, gorgeous beaches, and active cultural scene, is a location that encapsulates the spirit of Corsica. Whether you're sunbathing on its sun-kissed beaches, roaming its historic alleyways, or immersing yourself in its colorful festivals, Calvi provides a diverse Corsican experience that resonates with tourists from all corners of the globe. It's a village where beauty meets history on the Corsican coast, producing amazing experiences with every visit.

BONIFACIO

Bonifacio is located on the southernmost tip of Corsica. This essay will take you on a tour through its stunning cliffs, rich history, colorful culture, and fascinating sights.

Nestled near the southern point of Corsica, the town of Bonifacio is nothing short of a masterpiece sculpted by nature and history. Perched on spectacular limestone cliffs that overlook the glittering Mediterranean Sea, Bonifacio provides a spellbinding blend of beautiful surroundings, historical heritage, and a lively, friendly culture that draws guests to discover its every element.

Bonifacio's Culture and Language
Bonifacio's culture is a dynamic combination of Corsican customs and Mediterranean influences.
Local Language: While French is the official language, Corsican (Corsu) is both spoken and treasured. It represents the town's strong cultural identity.

Historical landmarks, museums, and must-see attractions
Bonifacio's most outstanding feature is certainly its stunning limestone cliffs, fashioned by nature over millennia. These towering promontories provide a striking backdrop for the

town. Bonifacio is not simply a refuge for nature aficionados; it's also rich in history that spans millennia.

Bonifacio features a coastline that is a dream come true for beach lovers and watersports enthusiasts.

- Cliffs of Bonifacio: The sight of these magnificent cliffs plummeting precipitously into the blue sea is awe-inspiring. The town's historic castle seems to dangle perilously on the edge, affording amazing views over the Bonifacio Strait and the island of Sardinia in the distance.

- Old Town and Citadel: The medieval old town of Bonifacio, with its tiny winding alleyways, is a living witness to the town's historical significance. Explore the citadel, see its museums, and stroll around the town's defenses for a voyage back in time.

- Stella Maris Church: The town's oldest church, Stella Maris, dates back to the 12th century. Its simple front covers a wonderfully designed interior that highlights Corsican religious art.

- Beaches of Bonifacio: Cala Longa, Plage de la Tonnara, and Rondinara are just a few of the magnificent beaches of Bonifacio. The crystal-clear seas and beautiful sands welcome you to sunbathe, swim, and enjoy the Mediterranean atmosphere.

- Boating and Watersports: Explore secret coves and sea caves on boat trips, or enjoy snorkeling, diving, and windsurfing in the beautiful seas that surround Bonifacio.

Festive Moments and Celebrations

- Cultural Festivals: Bonifacio offers different cultural events and festivals throughout the year. Be careful to match your visit with local events, which frequently involve traditional music, dance, and gastronomic pleasures.

- Corsican Polyphonic Singing Festival: This yearly event, normally held in September, brings together Corsican choirs and foreign ensembles to commemorate the island's rich musical legacy.

- Fête de la Saint-Julien: Held in August, this local event offers traditional Corsican music, dance, and a vibrant parade through the old town.

Culinary Delight

Corsican cuisine takes center stage in Bonifacio, giving a delectable trip through the island's tastes.

- Seafood Delights: With its seaside position, Bonifacio is known for its seafood. Sample fresh catches including sea urchins, lobster, and prawns, all served with a Mediterranean twist.

- Local Specialties: Savor Corsican delicacies such as "civet de sanglier" (wild boar stew), "brocciu"

(Corsican cheese), and charcuterie like "lonzu" and "figatellu."

Getting Around

- Walking: Bonifacio's tiny size makes it excellent for exploring on foot. Wander the old town's convoluted streets and soak in its antique splendor.

- Bicycles and scooters: Rent a bicycle or scooter to explore the town and its gorgeous environs at a leisurely pace.

- Automobile Rentals: If you prefer to drive farther into the Corsican countryside, automobile rentals are widely accessible, allowing you to discover the island's different areas.

Accommodation options

Bonifacio provides a choice of lodging alternatives, from sophisticated hotels to small guesthouses.

- Hotels: Enjoy a superb stay in beachside hotels like Hotel Genovese or Hotel Version Maquis. These provide breathtaking vistas and top-notch facilities.

- Boutique Inns & Guesthouses: Consider lovely boutique inns and guesthouses for a more customized experience. They frequently give an insight into Corsican hospitality and local traditions.

Bonifacio, where history meets natural wonder, is an invitation to immerse yourself in the varied fabric of Corsica's beauty and culture. Whether you're standing in awe of its towering cliffs, wandering its old alleyways, or indulging in its excellent food, Bonifacio gives a look into the heart and soul of Corsica. It's a community that embodies the soul of this magnificent island, allowing guests to have experiences that will last a lifetime.

CORTE

Known for its rugged surroundings, historical significance, and vibrant Corsican culture, Corte is a mesmerizing location that provides a distinct Corsican experience.

Nestled in the rocky center of Corsica, Corte is a village that defines the island's spirit. Surrounded by towering mountains and graced with an ancient fortress, Corte is a destination where nature and history mix to create a thrilling trip for anyone looking to understand the Corsican soul. Corte's biggest attractiveness comes from its wonderful natural surroundings.

Corte's Culture and Language
Corte is the birthplace of Corsican culture, where customs, music, and language are honored.

- Corsican Language: While French is the official language, Corsican (Corsu) has a unique place in the hearts of the residents. You'll commonly hear both languages in daily talks and observe Corsican street signs.

Historical landmarks, museums, and must-see attractions

- Corsican Mountains: The town is set in the central mountain range of Corsica, giving unique chances for trekking and outdoor excursions. Traverse the Gr20, one of Europe's most grueling long-distance routes, which passes through Corte, allowing access to spectacular vistas.

- Restonica Valley: A short drive from Corte, this lovely valley has clear mountain streams, rich forests, and dramatic granite cliffs. It's a hiker's dream, with routes that lead to tranquil lakes and spectacular overlooks.

Corte is not merely a natural beauty but also a hub of historical and cultural value.

- Fortress of Corte: The town's ancient fortress, built on a rocky hill, is a monument to its historical significance. Explore the citadel's cobblestone alleyways and visit the Museum of Corsica, which gives insights into the island's rich history, culture, and art.

- Birthplace of Paoli: Corte is commonly referred to as the "City of Paoli" because of its link with Pasquale Paoli, a crucial figure in Corsica's war for independence. Learn about this prominent Corsican statesman and his role in molding the island's history.

Festive Moments and Celebrations

Corte comes alive during its festivals, providing a look into Corsican traditions and an opportunity to rejoice alongside the people.

- Cultural Activities: Corte offers different cultural events, festivals, and exhibits throughout the year, allowing a chance to immerse oneself in Corsican traditions and modern art.

- Food Festivals: Time your visit with Corsican food festivals, where you may indulge in local delicacies and explore the island's gastronomic traditions.

- Fête de San Petru:** Held in late June, this festival honors Saint Peter, the patron saint of Corte. Enjoy parades, traditional music, and the colorful atmosphere.

- Corsican Music Festivals:** Various music festivals exhibit the island's rich musical tradition, including Corsican polyphonic singing and current music events.

Culinary Delight

Corsican cuisine takes center stage in Corte, giving a fascinating voyage through the island's tastes.

- Local Specialties: Savor Corsican cuisine like "civet de sanglier" (wild boar stew), "brocciu" (Corsican cheese), and charcuterie treats such as "lonzu" and "figatellu."

Getting Around
Corte provides a choice of transportation alternatives to explore the town and its gorgeous surroundings.

- Walking: Corte's tiny size makes it excellent for exploring on foot. The town's ancient streets and inviting ambiance promote leisurely strolls.

- Bicycles and scooters: Rent a bicycle or scooter to explore Corte and its lovely environs at your own leisure.

- Automobile Rentals: For those who prefer to explore further into the Corsican wilderness, automobile rentals are widely accessible, offering access to the island's different areas.

Accommodation Options
Corte has a selection of housing alternatives to accommodate varied interests and budgets.

- Hotels: Choose from a choice of hotels, from lovely boutique alternatives to warm family-run facilities. Some popular possibilities are the Hotel Dominique Colonna and the Hotel Duc de Padoue.

- Guesthouses and Inns: Consider staying in guesthouses and inns that give a warm Corsican welcome and insights into the island's culture.

Corte, with its awe-inspiring mountain vistas, historical riches, and vibrant Corsican culture, offers a unique and fascinating experience for guests. Whether you're hiking the Gr20, visiting the old fortress, eating Corsican cuisine, or immersing yourself in the town's cultural events, Corte gives a glimpse into the heart and soul of Corsica. It's a village where the raw nature of the island meets its rich history, generating memories that will linger with you long after your visit

PORTO-VECCHIO

Porto-Vecchio, a Corsican treasure, is famed for its magnificent beaches, active nightlife, historical charm, and Mediterranean allure. It is a place where history meets coastal beauty and modern sophistication.

Nestled along the southeastern coast of Corsica, Porto-Vecchio is a town that finds the right mix between ancient history, gorgeous beaches, bustling nightlife, and a rich Mediterranean environment. As one of Corsica's most popular locations, Porto-Vecchio draws guests with its numerous attractions, providing an amazing Corsican experience.

Historical landmarks, museums, and must-see attractions
Porto-Vecchio's most enticing feature is its gorgeous coastline and virgin beaches. Porto-Vecchio's beauty also goes beyond

its beaches, with historical treasures that take tourists back in time.

- Palombaggia Beach: Renowned as one of Corsica's most stunning beaches, Palombaggia enchants with its silky, white sands and crystal-clear waves. The environment is excellent for sunbathing, swimming, and water sports.

- Santa Giulia Beach: Santa Giulia's horseshoe-shaped bay is a gorgeous jewel, surrounded by green hills. The shallow, tranquil seas make it great for families and snorkeling aficionados.

- Rondinara Beach: This secluded beach is a hidden treasure, offering quiet beauty and pure blue waves. Rondinara is recognized for its distinctive form, like a scallop shell.

- Ancient Town (Citadelle): The ancient town is set on a hill and protected by medieval walls. Its small lanes, old buildings, and panoramic vistas make it a must-visit. Explore the bustling Place de la République, surrounded by cafés and stores.

- Gates and Fortifications: Discover the historic gates and fortifications that once safeguarded the town from attackers. The Porte Génoise and the Torra di Portivechju are outstanding examples of this architectural legacy.

Festive Moments and Celebrations

Porto-Vecchio comes alive during its colorful festivals, providing a taste of Corsican customs and an opportunity to rejoice alongside the people.

- Fête de Saint-Jean-Baptiste: Celebrated on June 24th, this festival comprises processions, traditional music, and exciting street celebrations in honor of Saint John the Baptist.

- Music Festivals: Various music festivals promote Corsican traditions, including polyphonic singing and modern music.

Vibrant Nightlife

Porto-Vecchio is also known for its active nightlife, with a profusion of pubs and clubs that come to life once the sun sets.

- Marina Nightclubs: The marina district is recognized for its sophisticated pubs and clubs, presenting a combination of Mediterranean refinement with Corsican charm. Sip beverages and dance beneath the stars as you enjoy the beach ambiance.

- Beach Parties: Many beach clubs organize nighttime events, providing a unique beachside party scene where you may dance with your toes in the sand.

Culinary Delight

Porto-Vecchio's eateries provide a delightful excursion into Corsican culinary heritage.

- Local Specialties: Indulge in Corsican cuisine like "civet de sanglier" (wild boar stew), "brocciu" (Corsican cheese), and charcuterie treats such as "lonzu" and "figatellu."

- Seafood Feast: Given its seaside position, Porto-Vecchio is known for its seafood. Savor oysters, prawns, and a variety of fresh seafood served with Mediterranean flair.

Getting Around

Porto-Vecchio provides many transportation alternatives for touring the town and its attractive environs.

- Walking: The town's modest size makes it excellent for leisurely exploration on foot. Stroll through its old streets and absorb the Mediterranean atmosphere.

- Bicycles and scooters: Rent a bicycle or scooter to enjoy Porto-Vecchio at your own leisure, allowing you to visit local sites.

- Vehicle Rentals: For those who desire to travel farther away or journey into the Corsican countryside, vehicle rentals are easily available, offering simple access to various sections of the island.

Accommodation Options

Porto-Vecchio provides a choice of hotel alternatives, from magnificent beachfront resorts to small guesthouses.

- Hotels: Choose from elegant waterfront hotels like Hotel Le Goéland and Hotel Casadelmar, offering breathtaking sea views and top-notch services.

- Boutique accommodations: boutique inns and small-scale accommodations give individualized experiences and an intimate setting.

- Guesthouses and Vacation Rentals: For a more domestic experience, choose guesthouses or vacation rentals, which frequently come with cooking amenities and an opportunity to connect with locals.

Porto-Vecchio, with its combination of seaside beauty, historical charm, active nightlife, and excellent food, provides a diverse Corsican experience. Whether you're lazing on its gorgeous beaches, discovering its old alleyways, or dancing the night away in its clubs, Porto-Vecchio encapsulates the spirit of Corsica, allowing you to make cherished moments that last a lifetime.

5. CORSICA'S ACCOMMODATION OPTIONS

Corsica provides a vast selection of lodging alternatives, from elegant coastal resorts to remote mountain refuges, guaranteeing that every tourist can find the appropriate location to stay while visiting this magnificent Mediterranean island. Corsica, an island of extraordinary beauty and different landscapes, welcomes guests with a broad selection of hotel alternatives, each delivering a distinct experience. From lovely beach hotels to isolated mountain getaways, the island offers something for everyone. Here are the categories of lodging possibilities accessible in Corsica:

1. Seaside Resorts

Corsica's coastline features various expensive coastal resorts that appeal to guests wanting a luxurious beachside experience. These resorts offer:

- Elegant accommodations: Enjoy comfortable and elegant accommodations with spectacular sea views.
- Private Beach Access: Many resorts feature private beach sections where you may unwind in privacy.
- Fine Dining: Savor wonderful Mediterranean and Corsican cuisine at on-site restaurants.
- Spa and Wellness: Indulge in spa treatments and wellness facilities to refresh the body and mind.

2. Boutique Hotels

For those who want a more private and customized ambiance, Corsica boasts a choice of boutique hotels. These provide:

- Unique Character: Boutique hotels are noted for their individual design and character.
- Local Experience: Immerse yourself in Corsican culture and friendliness.
- Tailored Services: Expect individualized care and attention to detail.

- Centrally Located: Many boutique hotels are situated in the core of Corsican towns, allowing easy exploration.

3. Vacation Rentals

Vacation rentals are a wonderful alternative for individuals who wish to live like locals. Options include:
- Apartments: Rent an apartment in a town or beach village for a domestic vibe.
- Villas: Larger parties can opt for a villa with private pools and spectacular views.
- Rural Retreats: Escape to secluded rural houses for a calm escape.

4. Guesthouses (Chambres d'Hôtes)

Experience Corsican hospitality at its finest by staying at guesthouses. These offer:
- Authentic Interactions: Connect with people and learn about Corsican traditions.
- Home-cooked meals: Many guest homes provide handmade Corsican meals.
- Personal Recommendations: Get exclusive ideas on the finest places to visit around.

5. Mountain Refuges

Corsica's rugged interior is peppered with mountain refuges, suitable for hikers and wildlife enthusiasts. They provide:
- Basic Accommodation: Expect modest facilities, including bunk beds and common dining spaces.
- Stunning Locations: Mountain refuges are frequently placed in secluded, scenic surroundings.

- Hiking Access: Use them as a base for exploring the island's hiking routes.

6. Camping and Glamping
Corsica is a sanctuary for campers and glampers. Options include:
- Campsites: Campsites are numerous, typically hidden in lovely areas along the ocean.
- Glamping Tents: Enjoy the outdoors with enhanced comfort in glamping lodgings.
- Stunning Night Skies: Corsica's isolated locations provide some of Europe's greatest astronomy.

7. Youth Hostels
For budget-conscious visitors and backpackers, Corsica provides a network of youth hostels. These provide:
- Affordable rates; Stay in dormitory-style or private rooms at budget-friendly costs.
- Social Atmosphere: Hostels regularly provide events and activities, making it simple to meet fellow travelers.

8. Bed and breakfasts
Experience Corsican culture and friendliness by staying at a bed and breakfast. These offer:
- Homely Atmosphere: Enjoy warm rooms and delicious Corsican breakfasts.
- Local Insights: Hosts may give vital insights into the island's hidden beauties.

9. Remote Cabins and Eco-Lodges

Eco-conscious guests might select secluded cottages and eco-lodges that offer:

- Eco-Friendly Stays: Stay in tune with Corsica's natural beauty.
- Unplugged Experience: Disconnect from contemporary distractions and appreciate the solitude of the woods.

10. Monasteries and Religious Retreats

For a unique experience, try staying at a monastery or religious retreat. These provide:

- Spiritual Retreats: Embrace solitude and introspection in tranquil places.
- Basic Accommodations: Expect simplicity and opportunity for reflection.

Whether you desire the richness of a beachside resort, the charm of a boutique hotel, the authenticity of a guesthouse, or the rustic simplicity of a mountain hideaway, Corsica's lodging choices ensure that your time on this gorgeous island will be nothing short of amazing. So, select the style that matches your interests and immerse yourself in the beauty and culture of Corsica.

6. CUISINE AND DINING

Corsica's food is a tantalizing voyage into the heart of Mediterranean delicacies, with a rich culinary legacy that reflects its distinct history and culture. Let's enjoy Corsican cuisine and dining, where traditional recipes, fresh ingredients, and a combination of influences come together to produce a memorable gourmet experience.

Corsica provides a gourmet excursion that is as enchanting as its landscapes. Corsican cuisine is a gastronomic journey through the island's rich history and different influences. From the mountains to the sea, Corsican meals are a savory mosaic of local products, fragrant herbs, and cultural traditions.

1. Mediterranean Flavors
At the core of Corsican cuisine lies the essence of the Mediterranean. Fresh and locally sourced ingredients take center stage in every meal. The island's beautiful waters supply an abundance of fish, while its rough topography provides an assortment of seasonal fruits, vegetables, and

fragrant herbs. Olive oil, a Mediterranean staple, fills meals with a rich and nutritious taste.

2. Wild Game and Charcuterie

Corsican cuisine embraces its hilly surroundings with dishes utilizing wild wildlife such as pigs and deer. Wild boar, in particular, is a Corsican delicacy commonly served as "civet de sanglier," a robust stew that displays the island's rustic qualities. The craft of charcuterie is a beloved heritage in Corsica, creating sausages, ham, and terrines that are second to none. "Lonzu" and "figatellu" are among the most recognized charcuterie treats.

3. Corsican Cheese

Cheese aficionados can discover joy in Corsica's peculiar cheese, "brocciu." This fresh, creamy cheese is a cornerstone of Corsican cuisine. It's used in a range of cuisines, from savory pastries like "fiadone" to pasta fillings and sweets. The island's cheesemakers also produce a selection of tasty kinds, each delivering a distinct taste of Corsican terroir.

4. Seafood Extravaganza

Given Corsica's coastal position, it's no wonder that seafood plays a big role in the island's cuisine. Fresh catches, including sea bream, sea urchins, lobster, and prawns, are masterfully cooked to accentuate their inherent tastes. Coastal eateries provide a magnificent array of seafood meals, from grilled fish to seafood stews.

5. A Blend of Influences

Corsican cuisine is a unique combination of Mediterranean, Italian, and Corsican elements. Its Italian link is obvious in dishes like "pasta ai frutti di mare," displaying Corsica's seafood riches. The island's pizza, nicknamed "pizzaiola," provides a fresh spin on the Italian staple.

6. Corsican Wines

No Corsican meal is complete without a glass of local wine. Corsica is home to various vineyards producing high-quality wines. The island's wine culture includes "Patrimonio" and "Ajaccio," famed for their red wines, and "Muscat du Cap Corse," a sweet and fragrant dessert wine.

7. Dining in Corsica

Dining in Corsica is an experience that marries the charm of local eateries with the sophistication of gourmet establishments. Whether you're eating a meal in a rustic mountain inn, a seaside tavern, or an exquisite coastal restaurant, the island's culinary riches are ready to be experienced.

8. Corsican Cafés

Corsican cafés, known as "café-paillotes," offer a relaxing setting for sipping espresso and savoring pastries. These lovely cafés are excellent for people-watching and engaging in local life.

9. Local Markets

Corsican markets are a culinary wonderland, where you may discover fresh vegetables, local cheeses, charcuterie, and handmade items. Don't miss the opportunity to try and purchase Corsican delights from friendly merchants.

10. Casual Eateries
Coastal towns and villages are peppered with casual eateries and seaside shacks that serve fresh seafood, pizzas, and plain Corsican fare. These restaurants are great for a laid-back dinner with a view.

11. Gourmet Dining
Corsica features a variety of gourmet restaurants, serving enhanced Corsican cuisine that exhibits the island's culinary talent. The ambience and service are as stunning as the cuisine.

Corsican cuisine is more than simply a meal; it's an opportunity to immerse yourself in the island's culture, history, and natural beauty. With its distinct combination of tastes, fresh ingredients, and a hint of Mediterranean appeal, Corsican cuisine delivers a sensory trip that makes a lasting impact on every traveler's palette.

TRADITIONAL CORSICAN DISHES

Traditional Corsican cuisine is a gastronomic tapestry fashioned from the island's rich history, different landscapes, and a blend of Mediterranean, French, and Italian influences. Here are some typical Corsican meals and elements that constitute the island's traditional cuisine:

1. Corsican Charcuterie

- Lonzu is a dry-cured pig loin that is a Corsican delicacy.

- Figatellu is a delicious liver sausage frequently served grilled or in stews.

- Prisuttu: Corsican ham, generally aged and seasoned with local herbs.

2. Civet de Sanglier: a robust wild boar stew that represents Corsica's hilly topography and affection for game meats.

3. Brocciu: a fresh, creamy cheese produced from sheep or goat's milk, widely used in both sweet and savory recipes.

4. Cannelloni au Brocciu: cannelloni pasta tubes stuffed with brocciu cheese, herbs, and occasionally a hint of lemon zest, then baked with a tomato sauce.

5. Fiadone: A Corsican cheesecake prepared with brocciu, sugar, and lemon zest, commonly served as a dessert.

6. Pâtes au Brocciu: Pasta, such as ravioli or lasagna, loaded with Brocciu cheese and herbs and served with tomato sauce.

7. Soupe Corse: A typical Corsican soup cooked with brocciu, mint, and citrus zest, delivering a pleasant and distinctive flavor.

8. Corsican Seafood: Corsica's coastal districts offer a plethora of fresh seafood, including sea bream, sea urchins, lobster, and prawns. Grilled or stewed, seafood dishes are a seaside delicacy.

9. Beignets de Brocciu: deep-fried fritters made with brocciu cheese and seasoned with a dash of sugar or citrus, producing a wonderful sweet delicacy.

10. Corsican Wines: Corsica is famed for its wine production. "Patrimonio" and "Ajaccio" give outstanding red wines, while "Muscat du Cap Corse" is a sweet and fragrant dessert wine.

11. Chestnuts: Corsican cuisine utilizes chestnuts in numerous forms, notably as flour for bread, pancakes (called "castagnacci"), and in stews.

12. Corsican Olive Oil: High-quality olive oil produced on the island enriches the tastes of Corsican meals.

13. Corsican Honey: The island's wildflowers and aromatic plants contribute to the particular tastes of Corsican honey, used in both sweet and savory cuisines.

14. Corsican Myrtle Liqueur: Myrtle liqueur, or "liqueur de myrte," is a traditional Corsican digestif prepared from the aromatic myrtle shrub.

15. Corsican Chestnut Beer: Corsica's chestnuts are utilized to produce chestnut beer, a unique and local beverage.

16. Corsican Herbs: Corsican cuisine relies on aromatic herbs like thyme, rosemary, and mint, which are used to infuse dishes with a delicious Mediterranean flavor.

17. Acquacotta: A basic vegetable soup with tomatoes, onions, and sometimes eggs, showing the utilization of fresh ingredients in Corsican cuisine.

Traditional Corsican cuisine is a delicious combination of fresh ingredients, fragrant herbs, and a deep connection to the island's natural wealth. It's a celebration of Corsica's rich history and cultural influences, delivering a unique and savory experience for anybody who travels to try its cuisine.

LOCAL FOOD MARKETS

Corsica features a dynamic network of local food markets where you can immerse yourself in the island's culinary traditions, sample fresh vegetables, and connect with friendly traders. Here are some significant local food markets in Corsica:

1. Ajaccio Market: Located in Corsica's capital, Ajaccio, this lively market provides a broad selection of items, from fresh fruits and vegetables to local cheeses, charcuterie, and seafood. It's a terrific site to experience the island's gastronomic wonders.

2. Bastia Market: Bastia's market, located in Place Saint-Nicolas, is one of the island's largest and most active. It provides a diversity of local items, including cheese, honey, meats, and fresh seafood. The market is a bright and pungent event, giving tourists a taste of Corsican culture.

3. Porto-Vecchio Market: Porto-Vecchio's weekly market, nestled in the town's historic center, provides a range of local food goods, crafts, and apparel. It's a terrific area to explore and find original Corsican products.

4. Calvi Market: Calvi's market, near the town's citadel, is famed for its fresh fish, Corsican cheeses, and dynamic atmosphere. It's a fantastic area to try local dishes and mingle with the friendly merchants.

5. Bonifacio Market: This market, nestled within the walls of Bonifacio's ancient town, is noted for its fresh food and interesting goods. You'll discover local cheeses, charcuterie, and handcrafted products that represent the town's rich culture.

6. Corte Market: The major market in Corte provides a range of regional cheeses, charcuterie, and Corsican wines. It's a must-visit when touring the heart of Corsica.

7. L'Île-Rousse Market: Set in the charming village of L'Île-Rousse, this market is a treasure trove of fresh Corsican food, including olive oils, jams, and aromatic herbs.

8. Propriano Market: Propriano's market boasts a delicious choice of local culinary goods, from freshly caught fish to handcrafted cheeses. It's an excellent spot to try Corsican cuisine.

9. Saint-Florent Market: Saint-Florent's market offers a true Corsican experience, with vendors selling local honey, charcuterie, and wines. It's a perfect stop while exploring the town.

10. Sartène Market: Sartène's weekly market is recognized for its colorful atmosphere and a selection of Corsican specialties. You may experience regional cheeses, fruits, and more in a lovely environment.

When visiting Corsican food markets, don't forget to mingle with the people, try the island's delicacies, and absorb in the colorful ambience. These markets provide a genuine experience of Corsica's culinary heritage and provide an opportunity to take home some of the island's exquisite delicacies.

DINING ETIQUETTES

Dining in Corsica is a pleasant experience, and while the mood is generally informal and convivial, it's necessary to be aware of certain dining etiquette to show respect for Corsican culture. Here are some dining etiquette recommendations to keep in mind when having a meal in Corsica:

1. Reservations
It's a recommended habit to make reservations, especially at famous restaurants, to reserve your table, especially during busy tourist seasons.

2. Punctuality

Arriving on time is appreciated. Corsican restaurants, like those in many Mediterranean cultures, frequently follow a slow pace, so leave yourself plenty of time to enjoy the meal.

3. Greetings

When entering a restaurant, greet the employees with a courteous "Bonjour" (good morning) or "Bonsoir" (good evening), depending on the time of day. It's considered respectful to recognize the people around you.

4. Dress Code

Corsicans normally dress casually for meals; however, at certain upmarket places, it's necessary to wear smart casual. Beach dress is not suited for upscale eating locations.

5. Table Manners

Corsicans respect good table manners. Keep your elbows off the table, hold your knife and fork properly, and chew with your lips closed. It's polite to wait until the host or the eldest member at the table begins the meal.

6. Tipping

A service fee is typically included in the bill. However, it's traditional to offer a tiny gratuity, either rounding up the whole cost or adding an extra 5–10%. If service is great, you may be extra generous.

7. Enjoying wine

Corsica is recognized for its wine; therefore, it's normal to drink a glass with your dinner. Allow your host to pick the wine or ask for recommendations from the staff. Don't fill your own glass; wait for someone to volunteer to do it for you.

8. Local food

Corsican food is a source of pride, and residents enjoy guests who show an interest in eating traditional dishes. Be open to tasting local specialties like wild boar, brocciu cheese, and charcuterie.

9. Local Customs

 Corsicans regularly share meals with people at the table. It's normal to provide a taste of your food or accept a taste of someone else's. This sharing is considered a show of kindness.

10. Language

While French is commonly spoken, people enjoy it when visitors make an attempt to speak some basic Corsican words. A simple "bon appétit" (enjoy your dinner) is always a wonderful gesture.

11. To-Go Boxes

It's not typical to ask for a to-go box in Corsican eateries. It's more customary to complete your dinner at the restaurant.

12. Slow dining

Corsican lunches are often unhurried events. Enjoy your food, engage in conversation, and take your time. Rushing through a meal is not the Corsican way.

By obeying these dining etiquette norms, you'll have a more pleasurable and culturally enlightening eating experience in Corsica. The island's friendly and hospitable residents enjoy tourists who show an interest in their culture and food.

7. ACTIVITIES AND ATTRACTIONS

Corsica, the "Island of Beauty," provides a broad selection of activities and attractions that cater to varied interests, from nature aficionados and history fans to adventure seekers and beach lovers. Here are some of the best activities and attractions in Corsica:

BEACHES AND WATERSPORT

Corsica is a heaven for beach lovers and water sports aficionados, with its crystal-clear waters, smooth sands, and a vast selection of activities to enjoy. Here are some of the top beaches and water activities in Corsica:

Beaches:

1. Palombaggia Beach: Known for its magnificent beauty, this beach offers fine white sand and brilliant blue waves, making it one of Corsica's most famous and gorgeous beaches.

2. Santa Giulia Beach: A family-friendly beach with shallow, calm seas and a crescent-shaped harbor. It's great for swimming and water sports.

3. Rondinara Beach: This gorgeous cove resembles a scallop shell and offers a calm ambience. The shallow, crystal-clear waters make it perfect for snorkeling.

4. Saleccia Beach: Accessible by boat or a 4x4 car, this beach is hidden in the Agriates Desert and is noted for its secluded and unspoiled beauty.

5. Ostriconi Beach: A long sandy beach with a wild and natural environment, suitable for those wishing to escape the throng.

6. Calvi Beach: Located near the town of Calvi, this beach provides a combination of water sports, swimming, and beachside eateries.

7. Propriano Beach: Propriano's beach is perfect for water activities like windsurfing and snorkeling. It's supported by a nice village with restaurants and stores.

8. Porto-Vecchio Beaches: This area features numerous gorgeous beaches, including Santa Giulia, Palombaggia, and Pinarello Beach, each with its own particular beauty.

Water Sports:

1. Snorkeling: Corsica's clean seas are great for discovering underwater life. Many beaches provide snorkeling possibilities, especially near rocky outcrops and coves.

2. Scuba Diving: Corsica is an excellent scuba diving destination with a variety of dive locations, including coral reefs, shipwrecks, and underwater caverns.

3. Sailing: Enjoy sailing along the Corsican coast, and you can even rent a sailboat or join a sailing trip. The island's protected coves and harbors are perfect for sailing.

4. Windsurfing: The island's constant breezes make it a good spot for windsurfing. The Gulf of Porto, in particular, is famed for windsurfing.

5. Kite Surfing: Try your hand at kite surfing in areas like Santa Giulia and Calvi, where the winds are excellent for this thrilling activity.

6. Jet Skiing: Jet skiing is accessible in numerous coastal areas, providing an exciting way to explore the shoreline.

7. Kayaking: Explore Corsica's craggy coastline and secret bays by kayaking. Guided trips are given for individuals new to kayaking.

8. Paddleboarding: Paddleboarding is a peaceful way to explore the island's calmer waters, and rentals are available at several beaches.

9. Boat Tours: Take a boat excursion to explore Corsica's coastline and visit isolated beaches and natural reserves, such as Scandola and the Lavezzi Islands.

10. Fishing: Join a fishing excursion to try your hand at catching the local seafood, or simply enjoy the pleasure of being out on the ocean.

Corsica's magnificent beaches and ample water activities make it a great vacation for anybody who likes sun, sea, and adventure. Whether you're seeking a quiet day at the beach or an adrenaline-pumping water activity, Corsica provides a number of possibilities for water aficionados.

HIKING AND OUTDOOR ADVENTURES

Corsica's various landscapes offer a paradise for hikers and outdoor lovers. Whether you're an expert mountaineer or a casual nature walker, the island has something for everyone. Here are some of the top hiking and outdoor activities in Corsica:

1. GR20: The GR20 is one of the most prominent long-distance hiking paths in Europe. It runs roughly 180 kilometers (112 miles) from Calenzana in the north to Conca in the south. The path takes you over tough mountain terrain, delivering challenging yet rewarding trekking with magnificent vistas.

2. Mare e Monti: This walk incorporates both sea and mountains, starting from Calenzana and going through varied scenery, including lovely towns, lush woodlands, and seaside trails.

3. Restonica Valley: Located near Corte, the Restonica Valley is a refuge for hikers. You may explore the valley's various routes, including the famed walk to Lake Melo and Lake Capitellu.

4. Bavella Massif: This location is noted for its distinctive rock formations and offers good chances for rock climbing and trekking. The Bavella Needles (Aiguilles de Bavella) are a notable attraction here.

5. Asco Valley: The Asco Valley is another trekking paradise with river gorges, thick woods, and the ability to discover high-altitude lakes.

6. Scandola Nature Reserve: Accessible by boat, this UNESCO World Heritage site gives an opportunity to explore unusual vegetation and animals, as well as spectacular cliffs and sea stacks.

7. Canyoning: Corsica's rivers and rugged topography make it an ideal place for canyoning. The island provides several canyoning excursions for all levels of experience.

8. Mountain bike: Corsica boasts a growing network of mountain bike routes. From seaside routes to rocky mountain tracks, the island is a terrific area to explore by bike.

9. Paragliding: Experience the exhilaration of flying over Corsica's magnificent landscapes with paragliding. You may discover paragliding centers in numerous areas of the island.

10. Horseback Riding: Discover Corsica's breathtaking splendor on horseback with guided riding trips that take you through woods, seaside routes, and hilly territory.

11. Corsican Nature Reserves: Explore the island's nature reserves, like the Bonifatu Forest and the Les Bouches de Bonifacio Nature Reserve, for unique ecosystems and animals.

12. Wild Swimming: Corsica is packed with natural pools, rivers, and waterfalls that are great for wild swimming and cooling off after a trek.

13. Via Ferrata: Corsica has various Via Ferrata routes, which are a combination of rock climbing and trekking, with steel ropes and ladders for extra thrill.

14. Geocaching: Enjoy the excitement of geocaching while experiencing Corsica's natural beauties. Many hidden caches may be located along hiking paths.

15. Multi-Day Treks: Beyond the GR20, Corsica provides a number of multi-day hiking possibilities, including the Mare a Mare routes and the Mare e Monti trails.

Corsica's rocky mountains, lush valleys, and stunning coastline provide a diversified playground for outdoor explorers. Whether you're seeking tough mountain climbs or quiet nature treks, Corsica offers plenty to offer hikers and outdoor enthusiasts of all abilities.

HISTORICAL SITES AND MUSEUMS

Corsica's rich past is represented in its historical sites and museums. From ancient ruins to landmarks of Napoleon

Bonaparte's early childhood, the island has lots to offer history aficionados. Here are some of the main historical sites and museums in Corsica:

Historical Sites:

1. Bonifacio Citadel: Perched on spectacular limestone cliffs, the Bonifacio Citadel is a magnificent medieval town that gives incredible views of the surrounding environment.

2. Corte Citadel: This medieval citadel was the birthplace of Pasquale Paoli, a major figure in Corsican history. The location has a museum and gives an insight into Corsican culture and tradition.

3. Filitosa Megalithic Site: Explore these prehistoric megaliths and sculptures, some of which date back to 1000 BC, and uncover Corsica's ancient history.

4. Calanche de Piana: This UNESCO World Heritage site is noted for its unusual rock formations and is a witness to the forces of erosion. Take a beautiful drive across the region to admire its geological splendor.

5. Genoese Towers: Throughout Corsica, you'll discover Genoese watchtowers that acted as lookout stations during the island's violent past. Many are well preserved and offer spectacular coastline vistas.

6. The Maison Bonaparte: Visit the birthplace of Napoleon Bonaparte in Ajaccio, which has been turned into a museum that gives insights into his early life and family.

7. Sartène: This quaint Corsican town is recognized for its medieval architecture and historic center, making it a great destination to roam and explore.

8. Aleria Roman Ruins: Discover the remnants of a Roman city, including a forum, hot baths, and a museum showing items from the site.

Museums:

1. Museé Fesch in Ajaccio: This museum offers one of the best collections of Italian paintings outside of Italy, as well as a range of Corsican art and antiques.

2. Musée de la Corse in Corte: Explore the island's culture and history via a diverse range of exhibits, including traditional Corsican costumes, utensils, and artwork.

3. National Museum of the Bonaparte Residence in Ajaccio: Housed in the historic home of the Bonaparte family, this museum dives into Napoleon's early life and legacy.

4. Corsican Museum in Bastia: Discover Corsican history and culture via a comprehensive collection of art, antiques, and displays.

5. Maison de la Photographie in Corte: Explore the visual history of Corsica through a collection of images chronicling moments from the island's past.

6. Prunelli Gorges Museum: Located in Tolla, this museum gives insights into the region's history, including its traditional activities and crafts.

7. Anthropology Museum in Corte: Learn about Corsica's culture and traditions via a comprehensive collection of ethnographic artifacts.

8. Corsican Prehistory Museum at Sartène: Discover Corsica's ancient past via artifacts and displays connected to the island's prehistoric ages.

Visiting these historical monuments and museums will allow you to immerse yourself in Corsica's enthralling past, from its ancient megalithic legacy to the early life of one of the world's most renowned personalities, Napoleon Bonaparte.

8. NATURE AND WILDLIFE

Corsica's various landscapes and abundant biodiversity make it a sanctuary for environmental and animal aficionados. The island provides a broad range of natural beauties, from beautiful beaches and lush forests to steep mountains and distinctive fauna.

CORSICAN NATIONAL PARKS

Corsica is home to many national parks and natural reserves, each giving a unique opportunity to explore the island's magnificent landscapes and various ecosystems. These protected areas provide a retreat for outdoor enthusiasts and wildlife lovers. Here are Corsica's important national parks and wildlife reserves:

1. Parc Naturel Régional de Corse (PNRC): Regional Natural Park of Corsica: This is Corsica's largest natural park and spans a substantial chunk of the island. It covers a diversity of landscapes, from coastal areas to alpine regions, making it a heaven for hikers and environmental aficionados.

2. Parc Naturel Régional de Corse - Sites Naturels de Scandola: A UNESCO World Heritage site, the Scandola Nature Reserve is recognized for its stunning coastal vistas,

including rocky cliffs, clean seas, and an abundance of marine life.

3. Parc Naturel Régional de Corse - Sites Naturels des Calanche de Piana: The Calanche de Piana is noted for its unusual red granite rock formations, high cliffs, and attractive vistas. It's an excellent area for trekking and boat cruises.

4. Parc Naturel Régional de Corse - Sites Naturels de Bonifacio: This component of the PNRC encompasses the Bonifacio region, allowing tourists an opportunity to experience the magnificent limestone cliffs and natural beauty of the area.

5. Réserve Naturelle de Scandola - Scandola Nature Reserve: Located inside the PNRC, the Scandola Nature Reserve is noted for its extraordinary maritime biodiversity, including uncommon fish species and seabirds.

6. Réserve Naturelle de l'Archipel des Lavezzi—Lavezzi Islands Nature Reserve: This reserve contains a collection of islands that are home to varied marine life and unusual flora species. It's a popular site for boat cruises and snorkeling.

7. Parc Naturel Régional de Corse - Sites Naturels de Bavella: The Bavella Massif is notable for its magnificent rock formations and hiking paths. It's a popular site for rock climbers and outdoor explorers.

8. Parc Naturel Régional de Corse - Sites Naturels de la Restonica: The Restonica Valley is a hiking and outdoor

paradise, with lush woods, alpine lakes, and a network of picturesque routes.

9. Parc Naturel Régional de Corse - Sites Naturels de les Aiguilles de Popolasca: The Aiguilles de Popolasca is a geological wonder with stunning rock formations that captivate geologists and nature enthusiasts.

These national parks and nature reserves in Corsica are carefully preserved to preserve the island's natural beauty and distinct ecosystems. They provide a wide selection of outdoor activities, from hiking and animal observation to water-based excursions. Whether you're exploring the harsh coasts, hiking into the hilly landscape, or finding the rich marine life, Corsica's national parks provide amazing experiences for nature aficionados.

BIRDWATCHING AND NATURE RESERVES

Corsica's numerous features, including mountains, woods, and coastal regions, make it a sanctuary for birdwatchers and environmental aficionados. The island is home to a variety of bird species, some of which are unique to Corsica. Here are some of the top sites for birding and natural reserves in Corsica:

1. Scandola Nature Reserve: This UNESCO World Heritage site is recognized for its beautiful shoreline and varied marine life. You may view a variety of seabirds, including gulls, cormorants, and the unusual Audouin's gull.

2. Lavezzi Islands Nature Reserve: These islands are a treasure for birdwatchers. You may view a number of seabirds, including the yellow-legged gull, the Mediterranean shag, and Cory's shearwater. The island's rugged cliffs provide nesting places for several species.

3. Réserve Naturelle des Bouches de Bonifacio: This nature reserve, which encompasses the strait of Bonifacio and neighboring territories, is a key stopover for migrating birds. It's an excellent place for observing numerous waterfowl, such as herons, egrets, and ospreys.

4. Restonica Valley: The wooded landscape of Restonica Valley gives possibilities for viewing woodland species, including numerous songbirds, woodpeckers, and birds of prey.

5. Bavella Massif: The rocky slopes and cliffs of Bavella are home to golden eagles, griffon vultures, and other birds of prey. It's an excellent site for birding against the backdrop of magnificent rock formations.

6. Corsican Nature Reserves: Various nature reserves in Corsica, such as the Bonifatu Forest and the Aitone Forest, are

good for birding. You may encounter Corsican nuthatches, warblers, and other forest-dwelling species.

7. Coastal Areas: Corsica's coastline provides homes for shorebirds and seabirds. Look out for oystercatchers, sandpipers, and gulls around the shorelines.

8. Corsican Wetlands: Wetland sites like the Biguglia Lagoon and the Etang de Palo are essential for waterbirds, particularly during migration. You may witness waders, ducks, and flamingos in these regions.

9. Corsican Scrublands and Maquis: The island's distinctive maquis, or scrublands, are home to various kinds of birds, including warblers, shrikes, and hoopoes.

10. Uccelluline Nature Reserve: Located on the island of Uccelluline, this reserve is dedicated to the conservation of seabirds and their habitats.

To really enjoy birding in Corsica, bring your binoculars and a field guide to Corsican bird species. Local birding trips and guides are also available to improve your bird watching experience. Whether you're visiting coastal locations, woodlands, or hilly terrain, Corsica provides a broad selection of birding chances for enthusiasts to discover the island's avian residents.

MARINE LIFE AND SCUBA DIVING

Corsica's crystal-clear seas and various marine ecosystems make it a superb location for scuba diving and studying marine life. The island's coastline parts provide a diverse underwater environment, containing colorful fish, interesting rock formations, and vivid coral.

1. Marine Life:
- Fish Species: Corsican waterways are filled with a variety of fish species, including grouper, bream, damselfish, and wrasse. You can also encounter octopuses, moray eels, and lobsters in the rocky crevices.
- Sea Turtles: Corsica's oceans are home to loggerhead and green sea turtles, giving them a spectacular sight for lucky divers.
- Dolphin and Whale Watching: While not guaranteed, it's possible to encounter dolphins, pilot whales, and even sperm whales on boat cruises off the Corsican coast.

2. Scuba Diving Sites:
- Réserve Naturelle de Scandola (Scandola Nature Reserve): Dive into the clean waters of this UNESCO World Heritage site to experience an underwater world replete with colorful marine life, caverns, and magnificent underwater scenery.
- Réserve Naturelle de l'Archipel des Lavezzi (Lavezzi Islands Nature Reserve): Known for its clean waters,

this reserve is a refuge for divers, with possibilities to view fish, sea urchins, and other underwater plants.

- Côte des Nacres (Coast of Nacres): This diving location in Porto-Vecchio offers good visibility and an opportunity to view diverse species, including conger eels and gorgonians.
- Rondinara Marine Reserve: This reserve near Bonifacio is noted for its sandy bottom and spectacular coral formations, attracting a diversity of fish and other marine species.
- Réserve Naturelle de Scandola (Scandola Nature Reserve): Dive into the clean waters of this UNESCO World Heritage site to experience an underwater world replete with colorful marine life, caverns, and magnificent underwater scenery.

3. Scuba Diving Centers: Corsica offers various scuba diving centers that offer guided dives, equipment rentals, and instruction for divers of all abilities. Some well-known diving centers are in Ajaccio, Porto-Vecchio, and Calvi.

4. Underwater Photography: Corsica's pristine seas and abundant marine life make it a fantastic place for underwater photography. Many dive facilities have photographers on staff who can record your underwater excursions.

5. Cave Diving: For more experienced divers, Corsica provides options for cave diving, with submerged caverns and tunnels to explore.

6. Shipwrecks: Corsica is home to a variety of shipwrecks, providing exciting diving locations. One of the most renowned wrecks is the General Leclerc near Bonifacio.

Diving in Corsica is a compelling experience, with an abundance of dive locations appropriate for both beginners and experienced divers. The island's mix of clean seas, rich marine life, and underwater scenery makes it a great location for anybody wishing to discover the secret world beneath the Mediterranean Sea.

9. CORSICAN CULTURE AND TRADITIONS

Corsican culture is a remarkable combination of Mediterranean and mountain traditions, influenced by the island's distinctive history, environment, and people. The culture of Corsica is a celebration of its rich past and particular way of life. Here are some features of Corsican culture and traditions:

LANGUAGE AND MUSIC

Language and music are two fundamental parts of Corsican culture, embodying the island's distinct character and traditions.

Language: Corsican, a Romance language closely linked to Italian, plays a vital part in Corsican culture.

1. Preservation of Corsican: While French is commonly spoken and understood, Corsicans are proud of their own language. Efforts are undertaken to preserve Corsican, which has numerous regional dialects. It's taught in schools, and there's a great drive to keep it alive.

2. sign of cultural identity: Corsican is more than simply a medium of communication; it's a sign of cultural identity. Speaking the language is a method for Corsicans to demonstrate their connection to the island's distinctive history and traditions.

3. Corsican Literature: Corsican literature has a long past, with poets and authors employing the language to tell stories, express emotions, and reflect on the island's history.

Music: Corsican music is recognized for its unusual polyphonic singing and traditional instruments.

1. Polyphonic Singing: Corsican polyphonic music, or "Cantu in paghjella," is notable for its multipart singing technique. Groups sing a cappella, producing harmonies and melodies that represent the island's history and agricultural life.

2. Famous Corsican artists: Corsica has produced renowned artists and ensembles, including A Filetta, I Muvrini, and the Chjami Aghjalesi. They've garnered an international reputation for their renditions of traditional Corsican music.

3. Lyrics and Themes: Corsican songs generally have lyrics that talk of Corsican identity, nature, love, and daily life. The themes represent the island's culture and customs.

4. Influence on modern music: Corsican music has had a considerable influence on modern music. The evocative harmonies of Corsican polyphony have influenced artists worldwide.

5. Musical Instruments: In addition to vocal music, Corsican culture also contains traditional instruments like the harp (a kind of guitar) and the pifana (a woodwind instrument).

Corsican music and language are strongly connected, with songs being utilized as a tool to portray Corsican national pride and history. The island's polyphonic music style, unique to Corsica, is a monument to the rich musical legacy of the region. Both language and music play a key part in conserving Corsica's cultural history and continuing its legacy for future generations.

LOCAL ARTISANS AND CRAFTS

Corsica has a strong legacy of craftsmanship and artisanal production, with local craftsmen making a diverse range of goods that represent the island's rich culture and traditions. Here are some of the local craftsmen and crafts you may explore in Corsica:

1. Pottery and Ceramics: Corsican potters manufacture a range of pottery pieces, including beautiful plates, bowls, and tiles. The ceramics generally contain traditional Corsican patterns and designs.

2. Corsican Knives: Corsica is famed for its knives, known as "couteaux Corses" or Corsican knives. These are manufactured with exceptional attention to detail and frequently have elaborate handles and high-quality blades.

3. Weaving and fabrics: Corsican artists make gorgeous fabrics using ancient techniques. You may get products such as tablecloths, napkins, and carpets with elaborate patterns.

4. Basketry: Corsican basket makers construct a broad variety of baskets, from useful containers to beautiful ones. These baskets are manufactured from natural materials such as wicker and may be found in many forms and sizes.

5. Woodwork: Local woodworkers in Corsica manufacture a range of wooden goods, including furniture, bowls, cutlery, and artistic carvings. Corsican chestnut wood is typically utilized for these constructions.

6. Corsican Cheese: Corsica is noted for its artisanal cheese manufacturing, notably the famed Brocciu cheese. Many small dairies and farms around the island produce this versatile cheese, used in numerous Corsican cuisines.

7. Honey and Beekeeping: Corsica's diversified landscapes provide an ideal habitat for beekeeping. Local craftsmen

manufacture high-quality honey, typically blended with distinctive flavors from the island's flora.

8. Essential Oils and Herbal Goods: Corsican artists manufacture essential oils and herbal goods utilizing natural flora. These things are valued for their fragrant and therapeutic characteristics.

9. Corsican Charcuterie: Corsican charcuterie is famous for its excellence. Local craftsmen manufacture exquisite cured meats, including lonzu (pork loin), coppa (pork collar), and figatellu (liver sausage).

10. Corsican Cosmetics: Corsica's natural resources, especially the famed Corsican myrtle, are employed in the manufacturing of cosmetics. You can buy a choice of skincare and cosmetics products that exploit the island's natural components.

11. Corsican Wine and Liquors: The island is home to various vineyards and distilleries that manufacture Corsican wines and liqueurs. Local winemakers employ local grape varietals to create distinctive and tasty wines.

When visiting Corsica, consider exploring local markets, artisan festivals, and craft shops to discover the work of these accomplished craftsmen. The goods they manufacture not only make for attractive and meaningful mementos but also give an insight into Corsican culture and workmanship.

CORSICAN FESTIVALS AND EVENTS

Corsica holds a number of festivals and events throughout the year, honoring the island's culture, customs, and dynamic way of life. These events give a terrific opportunity to immerse yourself in Corsican culture and experience the island's dynamic environment. Here are some of the best festivals and events in Corsica:

1. Calvi Jazz Event: Held in June, this event brings together jazz fans from across the world. Musicians play on open-air stages, making the most of Corsica's lovely weather.

2. Sea Festival in Bastia (Fête de la Mer): Taking place in July, this festival commemorates Corsica's marine history with boat parades, water-based competitions, and traditional music.

3. Porto Latino Festival: This music festival in St-Florent provides a broad roster of international and local musicians, making it a highlight of the Corsican summer festival calendar.

4. Festival d'Art Lyrique de Calvi: A classical music festival hosted in Calvi, where renowned performers play in a gorgeous outdoor environment.

5. Nuits de la Guitare in Patrimonio: A guitar event showcasing world-famous guitarists in a picturesque vineyard setting. It takes place in July and August.

6. Corsican Polyphonic Singing Festivals: Corsica is noted for its distinctive polyphonic singing. Various communities have singing festivals where Corsican choirs play their traditional music.

7. Les Rencontres de Calenzana: A contemporary art event in Calenzana that includes exhibitions, concerts, and performances during the summer months.

8. Semaine Napoléonienne in Ajaccio: A week-long series of activities commemorating Napoleon's legacy, including historical reenactments, parades, and fireworks. It takes place in August.

9. A Fiera di u Casgiu (The Cheese Event): This event in Venaco promotes Corsican cheese with tastings, music, and demonstrations of traditional cheese-making skills.

10. Feast of St. John the Baptist in Bonifacio: This yearly celebration in June features a parade, music, and dance to honor the patron saint of the city.

11. Bastille Day (Fête Nationale) in July: Corsica, like the rest of France, celebrates Bastille Day with fireworks, parades, and other events.

12. Assumption Day (L'Assomption) on August 15th: This Catholic festival is observed with processions and festivities in numerous cities and villages.

13. Christmas and New Year's Eve Celebrations: Corsica comes alive with festive lights, markets, and celebrations throughout the holiday season, especially in places like Ajaccio and Bastia.

14. Village Fairs: Many Corsican villages organize local fairs that incorporate traditional music, dance, and food, offering a true peek into Corsican culture.

These festivals and events give a unique opportunity to explore Corsica's cultural traditions, music, and food while enjoying the island's friendly and inviting ambiance. Whether you're interested in music, art, or local customs, Corsica has something for everyone to enjoy.

10. PRACTICAL TIPS FOR TRAVELERS

When traveling to Corsica, it's crucial to be well-prepared to make the most of your vacation. Here are some practical recommendations for travelers:

1. Weather and Clothing: Corsica has a Mediterranean climate, so bring light and breathable clothing for the warm summers. However, if you want to explore the mountains or travel during the colder seasons, pack clothing and suitable walking shoes.

2. Language: While French is frequently spoken, especially in metropolitan areas, learning a few basic Corsican words can be welcomed by locals and enrich your experience.

3. Currency: The official currency is the Euro (EUR). ATMs are readily available in towns, but it's a good idea to carry some cash, especially in rural settlements.

4. Transportation: Corsica's public transportation system is well developed. Consider hiring a car to explore rural locations, but be prepared for twisty mountain roads. Ferries are also a regular means to reach the island.

5. Outdoor Activities: Corsica is a wonderland for outdoor enthusiasts. If you plan on trekking, pack suitable clothing and be mindful of the difficulty level of your selected paths. If you're interested in water activities, such as scuba diving, consider carrying your own equipment if you have it.

6. Dining: Corsican food is a highlight of the trip. Don't miss the local delights like brocciu cheese, wild boar, and local wines. Make reservations at famous restaurants, especially during the high season.

7. Tipping: Tipping at restaurants is appreciated but not necessary. A 10% tip is usual, but check your receipt to see whether a service fee has already been added.

8. Shopping: Explore local markets and stores to locate handcrafted items. Many shops take credit cards, but it's a good idea to have cash for minor transactions.

9. Accommodation: Book lodgings in advance, especially during the busy summer months. Corsica provides a range of possibilities, from hotels to vacation homes.

10. Safety: Corsica is typically safe for vacationers, but be wary of your goods in crowded locations. Emergency services may be obtained by calling 112.

11. Respect local customs: Corsican culture places a significant premium on respect. Be respectful and consider asking permission before snapping photographs of individuals, especially in rural regions.

12. Local Events: Check the local calendar for festivals, as these might be a highlight of your vacation. Many of them are strongly established in Corsican culture and provide a unique experience.

13. Visit Local Artisans: Explore local artisan stores and support their work. Corsican workmanship is superb, and you may discover unique gifts.

14. Nature: Respect the environment, whether trekking or enjoying outdoor activities. Follow Leave No Trace guidelines and be cautious of fire threats, especially in the summer.

15. Language Barrier: While French is commonly spoken, Corsican is still dominant in some regions. Learning a few

simple Corsican words may go a long way in communicating with locals.

By keeping these practical recommendations in mind, you may have a more pleasurable and engaging experience while touring Corsica. This lovely island provides a diverse combination of culture, history, and environment, making it an intriguing destination for tourists.

SAFETY AND HEALTH

Safety and health are vital considerations for any tourist. Corsica is typically a safe vacation, but it's vital to be aware and prepared. Here are some safety and health considerations for your vacation to Corsica:
Safety:
1. Emergency Services: The emergency number in Corsica is 112. This number can be called for police, medical help, and fire emergencies.

2. Crime: Corsica has a low crime rate; however, small crimes, such as pickpocketing, can occur in popular tourist locations. Be cautious with your things, especially at prominent tourist sites.

3. Driving Safety: If you want to hire a car, be prepared for twisting mountain roads and tiny streets in some settlements. Drive carefully and stick to speed restrictions.

4. Fauna: Corsica is home to various fauna, including wild boars and mouflons. Be cautious when driving, especially at night, as animals may cross the road.

5. Outdoor Activities: If you engage in outdoor activities like hiking or water sports, observe safety recommendations and advise someone about your plans. Weather conditions can change fast, so check predictions before venturing out.

6. Fire Safety: Corsica is prone to forest fires, especially during the dry summer months. Follow any fire restrictions or warnings, and be aware of cigarette disposal in natural areas.

7. Water Safety: Be cautious when swimming or engaging in water activities, as currents and tides can be severe in some regions. Always observe safety requirements and pay heed to local warnings.

8. Health and Travel Insurance: Ensure you have comprehensive travel insurance that covers health emergencies, including medical evacuations, and any activities you plan to indulge in, such as hiking or water sports.

Health:

1. Medical Facilities: Corsica offers strong medical facilities and hospitals, especially in major towns and cities. Pharmacies are ubiquitous, and many pharmacists speak English.

2. Travel vaccines: Check with your doctor or a travel health clinic to determine if any vaccines or precautions are advised before traveling to Corsica.

3. Sun Protection: Corsica has lots of sunlight. Use sunscreen, wear a hat, and remain hydrated to protect yourself from sunburn and dehydration.

4. Insect Protection: In some regions, especially in the highlands, there might be insects like ticks. Consider applying insect repellent and checking for ticks if you've been in forested regions.

5. Food and Water Safety: Corsican cuisine is great, but it's necessary to maintain food and water safety. Stick to bottled water and dine at reputed businesses. Try local specialties, but be wary about hygiene.

6. Medical Kit: Pack a basic medical kit with necessities like painkillers, bandages, and any personal drugs you may require.

7. COVID-19: Stay current on any travel limitations or regulations relating to COVID-19. Follow local rules and be updated on the newest changes.

8. Travel Insurance: Consider obtaining travel insurance that covers medical emergencies and any outdoor activities you want to indulge in.

Corsica is typically a safe and healthy location, but like any trip, it's vital to be prepared and adopt common-sense safeguards. By following these guidelines, you may have a safe and happy vacation on this lovely Mediterranean island.

MONEY MATTERS

Managing your funds while vacationing in Corsica is a vital component of your trip. Here are some money-related ideas to help you negotiate your finances throughout your visit:

Currency: Corsica, like the rest of France, utilizes the Euro (EUR) as its official currency.

Cash and ATMs:
1. ATMs: ATM machines are commonly available in towns and cities around Corsica. You can withdraw cash in euros using your debit or credit card. However, it's a good idea to keep some cash on hand, especially if you plan to visit distant locations or tiny villages where ATMs may be less popular.

2. Banking Hours: Corsican banks normally follow conventional European banking hours, which means they may close for a few hours in the afternoon.

Credit Cards:
1. Acceptance: Credit cards, notably Visa and MasterCard, are extensively accepted in bigger towns and cities, including hotels, restaurants, and stores. American Express and other cards may be less often accepted.

2. Fees: Be aware of international transaction fees that your bank or credit card issuer may impose for using your card overseas. Check with your bank to understand these fees and consider selecting a card that offers travel advantages.

- Traveler's Checks: Traveler's checks have grown less common due to the availability of ATMs and credit cards. It's wise to carry several euros in cash as well as a credit card, as these are more readily accepted.

- Currency Exchange: You may exchange currency at banks and exchange offices in major towns and airports. Rates may vary, so it's a good idea to compare rates and fees.

- Tipping: Tipping is not necessary in Corsica, although a service charge is commonly included in restaurant bills. However, it's common to round up the amount or offer a little tip if you had good service. A 10% tip is welcomed, but you can change it based on your experience.

Budgeting:

1. Corsica is recognized for its exceptional food, which may be a big part of your spending. Plan your budget properly to enjoy local delicacies and dining experiences.

2. Consider the expense of outdoor activities and equipment if you wish to enjoy the island's natural splendor. Some activities may have related costs.

3. Accommodation rates vary based on the sort of housing you pick. Budget lodgings, holiday rentals, and campsites might be cost-effective solutions.

4. Keep in mind that Corsica, like many tourist locations, may have higher costs in popular regions and during busy tourist seasons.

Insurance: Consider getting comprehensive travel insurance that covers medical emergencies, trip cancellations, and any activities you plan to partake in, such as hiking or water sports.

Local Markets: Corsica features local markets where you may purchase fresh vegetables, handmade items, and unique souvenirs. It's important to have cash on hand for these transactions.

By being prepared and handling your expenses intelligently, you may enjoy a worry-free and pleasurable vacation to Corsica while making the most of your travel budget.

COMMUNICATION AND THE INTERNET

Staying connected and having access to the internet when traveling in Corsica is vital for communication and navigation. Here are some tips for communication and internet access:

Mobile Networks:
1. SIM Cards: Consider obtaining a local prepaid SIM card for your smartphone. Corsica has decent mobile network coverage, and this will provide you with a local phone number and data access.

2. Major Carriers: Corsica is served by major French carriers such as Orange, SFR, and Bouygues Telecom. You may locate their stores in larger towns and cities.

3. Service: Mobile service is normally high in metropolitan areas; however, it may be limited in isolated alpine locations or on certain beaches. Be prepared for intermittent signal dropouts.

Wi-Fi:
1. Wi-Fi in Accommodations: Most hotels, guesthouses, and vacation rentals offer Wi-Fi to guests. Ensure your accommodation provides this service if it's vital to you.

2. Restaurants and Cafés: Many restaurants, cafés, and bars provide free Wi-Fi to patrons. It's common to see signs offering "Wi-Fi gratuit."
Internet cafes: Internet cafes are not as widespread as they once were, but you may find them in bigger towns and cities.

Navigating Without Internet: If you want to explore rural locations without internet connectivity, try downloading offline maps or utilizing conventional paper maps to guarantee you don't get lost.

Language: French is the major language spoken in Corsica, and most individuals working in the tourism business speak some English. Learning a few simple French words may be beneficial and appreciated by locals.

Emergency Numbers: The emergency number in Corsica is 112, which you may call for police, medical help, and fire situations.

Internet Etiquette: When using public Wi-Fi or mobile networks, be cautious about accessing important information and consider utilizing a VPN for increased security. Public networks may not be as secure as private ones.

Roaming: If you want to use your home mobile phone number in Corsica, check with your cell operator regarding international roaming fees and data packages to prevent surprise expenses.

Communication Apps: Consider utilizing communication apps like WhatsApp, Skype, or Zoom for staying in touch with family and friends back home, since they may frequently provide cost-effective methods to make calls and send messages.

By following these recommendations, you can stay connected, use the internet, and communicate successfully while traveling in Corsica, guaranteeing a seamless and pleasurable journey.

11. RECOMMENDED ITINERARIES

Corsica offers a broad range of activities, from touring gorgeous towns in the highlands to resting on stunning beaches along the Mediterranean coast. Here are some recommended itineraries to help you make the most of your trip to this gorgeous island:

1. The Classic Corsica Adventure (7–10 Days):

Day 1-2: Bastia
Start your adventure at Bastia, Corsica's principal ferry port. Explore the ancient old town, tour the Citadel, and enjoy Corsican cuisine at local eateries.

Day 3-4: Cap Corse
Head north to Cap Corse, a craggy peninsula offering breathtaking coastal roads and lovely fishing communities like Nonza and Centuri. Hike to the lighthouse at Cap Corse for spectacular views.

Day 5-6: St-Florent
Continue south to St. Florent, a delightful town with stunning beaches and a vibrant marina. Explore the Agriates Desert and enjoy water sports.

Day 7-9: Calvi
Drive to Calvi, noted for its beautiful fortress and sandy beaches. Take a lovely train journey to discover the coast and relax by the water.

Day 10: Ajaccio
Head to Ajaccio, the birthplace of Napoleon Bonaparte. Visit museums and historical places, and discover the city's dynamic environment.

2. Mountain Adventures and Scenic Drives (7–10 Days):

Day 1-2: Ajaccio
Start your tour in Ajaccio, Corsica's capital. Explore the city and the historic places linked to Napoleon.

Day 3-4: Corte

Drive to Corte, a lovely mountain town and Corsica's cultural capital. Explore the historic town, climb in the Restonica Valley, and learn about Corsican history.

Day 5-6: Bastelica
Journey to the picturesque town of Bastelica in the Highlands. Experience traditional Corsican life and sample local food.

Day 7-8: Porto-Vecchio
Head to Porto-Vecchio on the eastern coast for lovely beaches and crystal-clear seas. Enjoy leisure, water sports, and local food.

Day 9-10: Bonifacio
Travel to Bonifacio, a spectacular seaside village set on rocks. Explore the historic town and take a boat cruise to appreciate the gorgeous shoreline.

3. Corsican Beach Escape (5-7 Days):

Day 1-2: Calvi
Start at Calvi, a lovely seaside town with sandy beaches. Relax on the beach, tour the Citadel, and enjoy water sports.

Day 3-4: Porto
Drive to Porto, a little fishing community with a lovely natural harbor. Take boat tours to visit the Calanques de Piana and Scandola Nature Reserves.

Day 5-6: Ajaccio

Head to Ajaccio and relax on the city beaches. Visit museums and immerse yourself in Corsican culture.

Day 7: Propriano or Bonifacio
Depending on your schedule, you can rest at Propriano with its stunning beaches or travel to Bonifacio for its spectacular cliffs and coastline splendor.

4. Hiking and Nature Discovery (10–14 Days):

Day 1-2: Calvi
Start your experience in Calvi and enjoy the city before going on your trekking journey.

Day 3-4: GR20 Trail
Begin the famed GR20 hiking path from Calenzana, a tough but rewarding walk through Corsica's magnificent mountains. Plan for numerous days on the trek.

Day 5-7: Corte
Arrive at Corte, the trail's midway point. Rest, visit the town, and take a side excursion to the Restonica Valley.

Day 8-10: Vizzavona
Continue your GR20 trek towards Vizzavona. Enjoy the lush forests and beautiful vistas along the route.

Day 11–14: Bonifacio
After finishing the GR20, treat yourself to leisure in Bonifacio and explore the stunning coastline cliffs.

These itineraries give a glimpse of the varied activities Corsica has to offer, whether you're interested in beach holidays, mountain adventures, cultural discovery, or hiking. Tailor your vacation to your tastes and enjoy this gorgeous Mediterranean island.

ONE-WEEK CORSICAN ADVENTURE

If you have one week to tour Corsica, you may focus on a combination of the island's spectacular natural beauty, historic attractions, and bustling coastal villages. Here's a one-week Corsican adventure itinerary:

Day 1: Arrival in Bastia
- Arrive in Bastia, Corsica's principal ferry port.
- Explore the ancient old town, see Saint-Nicholas Square, and eat your first Corsican dinner at a local restaurant.

Day 2: Cap Corse
- Take a day excursion to Cap Corse, a rough peninsula in the north.
- Visit lovely fishing communities like Nonza and Centuri.
- Hike to the lighthouse at Cap Corse for spectacular views.

Day 3: St-Florent
- Drive to St-Florent, a lovely seaside village.
- Spend your day enjoying the magnificent beaches, water sports, and visiting the busy marina.

Day 4: Calvi
- Continue your journey to Calvi, noted for its beautiful fortress and sandy beaches.
- Take a picturesque train trip along the coast to view the scenic magnificence.

Day 5: Calvi's Surroundings
- Spend the day exploring Calvi's environs.
- Visit the Calanques de Piana and the Scandola Nature Reserve for their unusual rock formations and pristine waters.

Day 6: Porto
- Travel to Porto, a little fishing community with a magnificent natural harbor.
- Take a boat tour to visit the Calanques de Piana and Scandola Nature Reserve.

Day 7: Departure from Ajaccio
- Drive to Ajaccio, Corsica's capital, for your departure.
- Explore the city, see the Napoleon Bonaparte museums, and eat your final Corsican supper.

This one-week tour delivers a taste of Corsica's various landscapes, ancient attractions, and coastline appeal. You'll enjoy magnificent beaches, craggy coasts, and lovely villages along the route, making the most of your brief vacation to this Mediterranean treasure.

FAMILY-FRIENDLY VACATIONS

Corsica is a superb place for a family-friendly holiday, offering a blend of stunning beaches, outdoor excursions, and cultural encounters. Here's a family-friendly itinerary for a one-week holiday in Corsica:

Day 1: Arrival in Bastia
• Arrive in Bastia and relax in your family-friendly hotel.
• Stroll through the ancient town, eat a leisurely meal, and absorb the Corsican atmosphere.

Day 2: Bastia Exploration
• Explore Bastia with the family. Visit the historic port, the Citadel, and the Bastia Market.
• Spend a leisurely afternoon at Arinella Beach, which is perfect for swimming and playing in the sand.

Day 3: Cap Corse Day Trip
• Take a family day excursion to Cap Corse. Enjoy picturesque drives along the coast and see lovely villages like Nonza and Centuri.
• Stop for picnics at stunning vistas and let the youngsters take in the wonderful surroundings.

Day 4: St-Florent Fun
• Drive to St. Florent, a family-friendly seaside town with wonderful beaches.
• Spend the day playing in the water, creating sandcastles, and enjoying different water activities.

Day 5: Scenic Train Ride to Calvi
• Take a picturesque train trip from St. Florent to Calvi. The youngsters will appreciate the wonderful coastline vistas.
• In Calvi, tour the old citadel and have ice cream or gelato on the shore.

Day 6: Calanques de Piana and Scandola Boat Tour
• Experience a boat journey to the Calanques de Piana and Scandola Nature Reserve. The distinctive rock formations and crystal-clear waterways will astonish both youngsters and adults.

Day 7: Relax in Porto
• Head to Porto, a peaceful beach hamlet. Enjoy a relaxed day by the sea, swimming, and visiting the harbor.
• Consider a boat trip down the shore if the family is up for it.

Day 8: Adventure in Corte
• Drive to Corte, a lovely mountain village. Explore the historic town and take the family on a trek in the Restonica Valley.
• Kids may play in the cold mountain streams, making it a wonderful day for everybody.

Day 9: Corte and Corsican Traditions
• Spend the morning in Corte. Learn about Corsican culture and history at the Corsican Museum.
• In the afternoon, you may visit local artists and admire traditional Corsican crafts.

Day 10: Propriano Beach Day

• Drive to Propriano, a family-friendly coastal town.
• Spend your last day in Corsica lounging on the beach, swimming, and playing beach games.

Day 11: Departure from Ajaccio
• Drive to Ajaccio for your departure.
• Spend some time exploring the city, visiting museums, and having your final Corsican supper.

This family-friendly trip allows you to blend outdoor experiences with relaxing on the beach and discovering Corsica's cultural history. Corsica's natural beauty, great food, and inviting attitude make it a perfect choice for family vacations.

ROMANTIC GETAWAY

Corsica is an excellent place for a romantic trip, providing gorgeous landscapes, quiet towns, and exquisite restaurants. Here are some recommended romantic holiday alternatives for couples in Corsica:

1. Romantic Retreat in Calvi (4-5 Days):
• Spend your romantic holiday in the lovely village of Calvi.
• Explore the historic Citadel, which provides excellent panoramic views.
• Enjoy leisurely strolls on the sandy beach and bathe in the Mediterranean sun.
• Have a fantastic evening at one of the seafood restaurants along the waterfront.

2. Corsican Wine Tour (4-6 Days):
• Embark on a romantic wine trip, experiencing Corsica's vineyards and wine cellars.
• Visit renowned vineyards in locations like Patrimonio and Sartène.
• Savor wine tastings and match them with Corsican cheeses and charcuterie.
• Stay in lovely apartments among the vineyards and spend romantic nights beneath the stars.

3. Coastal Getaway in Porto-Vecchio (5-7 Days):
• Escape to the magnificent beaches of Porto-Vecchio.
• Relax on the lovely coasts of Palombaggia and Santa Giulia beaches.
• Take a boat cruise to discover the Lavezzi Islands and Bonifacio's stunning cliffs.
• Dine at coastal restaurants and taste fresh seafood while watching the sunset.

4. Mountain Romance in Corte (4-5 Days):
• Find romance in the Corsican Highlands by vacationing in Corte.
• Explore the Restonica Valley's natural splendor on treks and swim in mountain streams.
• Picnic beside the Tavignano River and feel the calm of the Corsican forest.
• Discover Corsican customs and craftsmanship with a visit to local craftsmen.

5. Secluded Beach Escape in Bonifacio (3–4 Days):
• Experience closeness in the isolated village of Bonifacio.

• Visit the ancient Old Town and enjoy a boat cruise to the spectacular adjacent sea caves.

• Enjoy private beach picnics and swim in crystal-clear seas.

• Savor a romantic supper at a cliffside restaurant overlooking the Mediterranean.

6. Ajaccio, the City of Love (4-5 Days):

• Explore the capital city, Ajaccio, with its charming ambience.

• Visit the boyhood home of Napoleon Bonaparte and the Fesch Museum.

• Wander the lovely neighborhoods and eat leisurely lunches at quiet restaurants.

• Enjoy the lovely city beaches and enjoy the sunsets over the Gulf of Ajaccio.

7. Adventure and Romance in Corsican Villages (6–8 Days):

• Travel through Corsica's lovely villages and landscape.

• Explore the mountain villages of Zonza, Sartène, and Piana.

• Discover hidden jewels, stroll picturesque trails, and sample local food.

• Stay in small bed and breakfasts and appreciate the quiet ambiance of Corsican life.

These romantic weekend ideas in Corsica allow you to discover the island's natural beauty, cultural legacy, and great food while making cherished memories with your loved one. Whether you like the beach, the mountains, or ancient villages, Corsica has something to offer every couple seeking romance and leisure.

12. USEFUL PHRASES AND VOCABULARY

Learning some basic Corsican phrases and terminology will enrich your trip and help you connect with the local culture. Here are some useful phrases and words:

Greetings:
- Bonjour! - Good morning.
- Bonsoir - Good evening
- Bonne nuit - Good night.

- Salut - Hi/Hello
- Comment ça va ? - How are you?
- Ça va bien, merci - I'm okay, thanks
- Enchanté(e) - Nice to meet you

Polite Expressions:
- S'il vous plaît - Please
- Merci - Thank you
- Merci beaucoup - Thank you very much.
- De rien - You're welcome
- Excusez-moi - Excuse me
- Pardon - Sorry
- Oui - Yes
- Non - No

Basic Conversational Phrases:
- Parlez-vous anglais ? - Do you speak English?
- Je ne parle pas très bien français - I don't speak French very well
- Pouvez-vous m'aider ? - Can you assist me?
- Je voudrais... - I would want...
- Où est... ?- Where is...?
- Combien ça coûte ? - How much does it cost?
- L'addition, s'il vous plaît - The check, please

Numbers:
- Un - One
- Deux - Two
- Trois - Three
- Quatre - Four
- Cinq - Five

- Six - Six
- Sept - Seven
- Huit - Eight
- Neuf - Nine
- Dix - Ten

Food & Dining:
- La carte - The menu
- Une table pour deux - A table for two
- L'entrée - Appetizer
- Le plat major - Main course
- Le dessert - Dessert
- L'eau - Water
- Le vin - Wine
- L'addition - The bill

Direction and Transportation:
- Gauche - Left
- Droite - Right
- Tout droit - Straight forward
- Arrêt de bus - Bus stop
- Gare - Train station
Aéroport-Airport

Time and Dates:
- Quelle heure est-il ? - What time is it?
- Aujourd'hui - Today
- Demain - Tomorrow
- Hier - Yesterday
- Matin - Morning
- Après-midi - Afternoon

- Soir - Evening
- Jour - Day
- Semaine - Week
Mois - Month
- Année - Year

Common Courtesies:
- S'il vous plaît, merci, and bonjour are widely used to convey respect and courtesy.

Shopping:
- Ouvrir - Open
- Fermer - Close
- Magasin - Shop
- Prix - Price

Learning these phrases and terms will be beneficial throughout your time in Corsica and will show your admiration for the local culture. Corsicans are often happy when tourists make an attempt to speak their language, even if it's just a few words.

13. ACKNOWLEDGMENTS

I would like to convey my thanks to the individuals and places who made this Corsica travel guide possible. It's been a voyage of discovery, and I couldn't have done it without the aid and support of many individuals and organizations.

I wish to thank the kind and inviting people of Corsica who offered their tales, expertise, and enthusiasm for this beautiful island. Your warmth and thoughtfulness have left an unforgettable impact on my heart.

I am truly thankful to the local companies, guides, and experts who kindly contributed their views and experiences, enabling me to build a thorough book that I believe will be a great resource for travelers.

I'd also like to express my appreciation to my family and friends for their constant support and encouragement during this effort.

14. AUTHOR'S NOTE

As the author of this Corsica travel guide, I began on a journey to experience the gorgeous scenery, rich culture, and warm-hearted people of Corsica. The objective was to develop a book that not only gives useful information for guests but also conveys the soul and character of this Mediterranean jewel.

Corsica is a site of great beauty, from the beautiful beaches to the harsh mountain scenery. Its past is famous, and its culture is distinct. It's my aim that this book will encourage you to immerse yourself in the wonder of Corsica, whether you're a seasoned traveler or someone experiencing the delights of adventure for the first time.

This book is a labor of love, and I hope it serves as a companion to your own Corsican experience. As you wander across this island, may you find the numerous treasures it possesses and build memories that will last a lifetime.

Happy travels,
Kiran McDonald.

Printed in Great Britain
by Amazon

44518937R00076